The Journal of the History of Philosophy Monograph Series
Edited by Richard H. Popkin and Richard A. Watson

Also in this series

*Shūzō Kuki and Jean-Paul Sartre: Influence and
Counter-Influence in the Early History
of Existential Phenomenology*
  Stephen Light

*The Scottish Enlightenment and the Theory of
Spontaneous Order*
  Ronald Hamowy

The Dream of Descartes
  Gregor Sebba

Kant's Newtonian Revolution in Philosophy
  Robert Hahn

Aristotle on the Many Senses
of Priority

By
John J. Cleary

Published for
The Journal of the History of Philosophy, Inc.

SOUTHERN ILLINOIS UNIVERSITY PRESS
Carbondale and Edwardsville

91 90 89 88   4 3 2 1

Library of Congress Cataloging-in-Publication Data

Cleary, John J.
Aristotle on the many senses of priority.

(The Journal of the history of philosophy monograph series)
"Published for the Journal of the History of Philosophy, Inc."
Bibliography: p.
Includes index.
1. Aristotle—Contributions in the concept of
priority.   2. Priority (Philosophy)—History.
I. Title. II. Series.
B491.P75C58   1988   110   87-32202
ISBN 0-8093-1465-7

For my wife, Breda

CONTENTS

THE *JOURNAL OF THE HISTORY OF PHILOSOPHY*
Monograph Series

THE *JOURNAL OF THE HISTORY OF PHILOSOPHY* MONOGRAPH SERIES, CONSISTING OF volumes averaging 80 to 120 pages, accommodates serious studies in the history of philosophy that are between article length and standard book size. Editors of learned journals have usually been able to publish such studies only by truncating them or by publishing them in sections. In this series, the *Journal of the History of Philosophy* presents, in volumes published by Southern Illinois University Press, such works in their entirety.

The historical range of the *Journal of the History of Philosophy* Monograph series is the same as that of the *Journal* itself—from ancient Greek philosophy to the twentieth century. The series includes extended studies on given philosophers, ideas, and concepts; analyses of texts and controversies; new translations and commentaries on them; and new documentary findings about various thinkers and events in the history of philosophy.

The editors of the Monograph Series, the directors of the *Journal of the History of Philosophy*, and other qualified scholars evaluate submitted manuscripts.

We believe that a series of studies of this size and format fulfills a genuine need of scholars in the history of philosophy.

Richard H. Popkin
Richard A. Watson
—Editors

PREFACE

THE PROBLEM THAT MOTIVATES THIS STUDY WAS GENERATED QUITE SOME TIME
ago when I was working on a dissertation about Aristotle's thought on the
foundations of mathematics and came across a passage in the *Topics* that
did not seem to fit with the anti-Platonism I had routinely assumed to be
characteristic of his views. In spite of the dialectical nature of the general
context, I was unable to explain away this puzzling passage or to reconcile it with passages in *Metaphysics* Mu that clearly rejected mathematical Platonism. The resultant state of puzzlement in which I found myself
proved to be fertile ground for the seeds of doubt about the standard account of Aristotle's intellectual development as a thinker with an inbuilt
prejudice against mathematics. But the development of an alternative
account is not an easy task and I am not satisfied that this has yet been ac-
complished. In fact, I am presently writing a book-length study that tries
among other things to give a comprehensive account of both the positive
and negative functions of mathematics in Aristotle's cosmological and
metaphysical thought. In the present monograph, however, I am under-
taking the more modest project of studying the different senses of 'priority' in his logical and metaphysical works. Apart from the intrinsic interest of the topic itself, such a study serves to focus our attention on the
characteristic way in which Aristotle both continues and breaks away
from the Platonic tradition.

Like everyone else who has worked on a project such as this, I have in-
curred all kinds of personal and intellectual debts that can never be fully
repaid. Though he may not always recognize the way in which his influence has worked on me, I think that my greatest intellectual debt is owed
to Hans-Georg Gadamer, who taught me (among many other things) to respect the ancient tradition about the unity of the Platonic-Aristotelian
problematic. I am also greatly indebted to my friend Donald Morrison
(who read an earlier version of this project and made many insightful criti-
cisms) for allowing me to read and cite his unpublished papers on
Aristotle's degrees-of-reality thesis. A similar debt is owed to John Rist for
allowing me to read and cite his unpublished manuscript on Aristotle's development. In addition, I would like to thank Hippocrates Apostle for giving me permission to use his fine translations of Aristotle's works. Finally,
I am deeply grateful to my colleague, Arthur Madigan, S. J., for carefully
checking all my translations from the Greek and for improving them

through his judicious suggestions. Of course, any errors made in this book are entirely my own responsibility.

I would like to thank the administration of Boston College for financial support in the form of a faculty research fellowship that freed me from teaching duties in the fall semester of 1986, thereby giving me the leisure to revise and prepare this monograph for publication. Finally, on a more personal note, I want to dedicate this book to my wife, Breda, whose love and moral support have been crucial for my well-being throughout the years of work and study that find their fruition here.

Aristotle on the Many Senses of Priority

ABBREVIATIONS

An.Pr.	*Prior Analytics*
An.Pst.	*Posterior Analytics*
Cat.	*Categories*
Comm. Math.	Iamblichus, *De Communi Mathematica Scientia Liber*
DA	*De Anima*
De Cael.	*De Caelo*
De Gen. An.	*De Generatione Animalium*
De Int.	*De Interpretatione*
De Part. An.	*De Partibus Animalium*
De Prim. Prin.	Duns Scotus, *Tractatus de primo principio*
EE	*Eudemian Ethics*
EN	*Nicomachean Ethics*
In An. Pst.	Commentaries on the *Posterior Analytics*
In Cat.	Commentaries on the *Categories*
In De Cael.	Commentaries on *De Caelo*
In Eucl.	Proclus, *Commentary on Euclid's Elements*
In Metaph.	Commentaries on the *Metaphysics*
In Phy.	Commentaries on the *Physics*
In Top.	Commentaries on the *Topics*
LSJ	Liddell, Scott and Jones, *A Greek Lexicon*
Met.	*Metaphysics*
Opus Oxon.	Duns Scotus, *Opus Oxoniense*
Protr.	*Protrepticus*
Parm.	*Parmenides*
Phaed.	*Phaedo*
Phaedr.	*Phaedrus*
Phil.	*Philebus*
Phy.	*Physics*
Pol.	*Politics*
Quodl.	Duns Scotus, *Quaestiones quodlibetales*
Rhet.	*Rhetoric*
Soph. El.	*Sophistical Refutations*
Sum. Log.	Ockham, *Summa totius logicae*
Theaet.	*Theaetetus*
Tim.	*Timaeus*
Top.	*Topics*

Introduction

ARISTOTELIAN COMMENTATORS[1] FROM ALL AGES HAVE USUALLY ACKNOWLEDGED
the thesis about the multiple senses of 'being' as a basic part of Aristotle's
claim to have made significant progress over his philosophical predecessors. In contemporary scholarship,[2] however, what is not adequately recognized is that this is closely related to an equally important thesis about the
many senses of 'priority,' which itself is crucial for his break with Platonism. Therefore, in this monograph I intend to explore the significance of
this latter thesis for the development of Aristotle's problematic about substance and the related question about the ontological status of mathematical objects. My point of departure will be a curious passage in the *Topics,*
where he appears to accept a schema of priorities that would make mathematical entities more substantial than sensible things.[3] Given his own categorical framework, such an implication represents a reversal of what are
taken to be Aristotle's standard views on substance. In order to make sense
of this, I will survey his treatment of priority in the *Categories,* while giving
special attention to the criterion for natural priority. Through a comparison with the more expansive treatment of priority in *Metaphysics* Delta, I
will try to show that at least some of the criteria are inherited from Plato.
Even though this systematic treatment lists many of the "ways" of priority
shared by his predecessors, it also facilitates Aristotle's basic claim that
substance is prior in every important sense.[4]

The final chapter of this book will attempt to work out some of the implications of this claim as they appear in parts of the *Metaphysics* and of the
Physics. In this way I hope to illustrate the importance of the concept of priority for understanding some of his most characteristic metaphysical positions. For instance, without attempting to resolve the problem, I will show
the relevance of priority to the perennial question of whether his first philosophy is "metaphysica generalis" or "metaphysica specialis."[5] Since
'being' is a *pros hen* equivocal, according to Aristotle, the crux of this issue
is how many kinds of substance there are and which is prior. In fact, as we
shall see from *Metaphysics* Lambda, he only admits one kind of substance
as being prior to sensible substance; i.e. what is described as having the
mode of being of a prime mover. I shall briefly examine the nature of that
priority and the arguments used to support it. Finally, with reference to Mu
2, I will return full circle to the question about mathematical objects, which
was raised initially by the *Topics* passage. I will argue that here we find

Aristotle implicitly rectifying his earlier mistake by distinguishing between two senses of priority that were previously conflated. While he concedes to the Platonists that mathematical entities are prior to sensible bodies "in formula" (τῷ λόγῳ), he denies that they are also prior "in substance" (τῇ οὐσίᾳ).

Given the prominent role of "the prior and the posterior" in many Aristotelian arguments, it is difficult to understand the relative neglect of this topic among modern scholars before and after Bretano[6] who have paid great attention to the many senses of being. Perhaps such neglect is due to the historical fact that hierarchical thinking was shunned by philosophers after their self-conscious break with medieval scholasticism. Be that as it may, however, I think it is unwise to ignore the presence of such thinking in Plato and Aristotle when they develop many of their characteristic philosophical positions.[7] A sociologist of ideas might even speculate that hierarchical thought was grounded in the social and political structures of ancient Greek society. While I am not going to pursue such speculation here, I think that some conceptual and philological support for it may be found in at least one of the senses of priority listed by Aristotle in the *Categories*. In the *Metaphysics* also he forges a conceptual link between that meaning of priority and the activity of a political or military leader (ἄρχων) whose decision is prior in the sense that it determines the action of followers. In that special sense, the decision is an ἀρχή or beginning of action and this has broader ramifications for the whole notion of first principle. Some of the mythical resonance of the question about "beginnings" (ἀρχαί) can still be heard in Plato and Aristotle when they ponder the mystery of beginnings in the universe and in thought. All this should be recalled while we are dealing with the prosaic topic of the different senses of priority.

Perhaps this is the best place to enter a caveat against a possible confusion of Aristotle's notion of priority with Kant's notion of *a priori*. The latter has a special meaning by contrast with *a posteriori* within an epistemological framework that is quite foreign to the thought of Aristotle, even when the latter is considering how we know necessary truths. While it may be the case that the terms "a priori" and "a posteriori" were originally derived from Aristotle by way of Scholastic thought,[8] it seems to me that Kant has radically changed their meaning with his epistemological presuppositions.[9] For instance, the claim that one can understand a concept or recognize the truth of a proposition independently of experience would hardly make any sense for Aristotle, even if we were to place it within the context of his opposition to Platonic ideas. After all, he does accuse of mere "twittering" those who talk about the Forms as if they were separated from the corresponding things in the sensible world that are supposed to imitate them or participate in them; cf. *An. Pst.* 83a33–36. Given his conception of passive *nous* as that which is capable of receiving all intelligible forms, it is clear that there is no place in Aristotle's epistemology for the notion that some concept might be grasped prior to all experience. But the decisive difference from Kant is that 'priority' for Aristotle is not merely an epistemological term, but rather that it has a range of meanings spanning his whole philosophy from logic to metaphysics. In view of our modern Kantian prejudices, I think that the many senses of priority in Aristotle need fresh scrutiny.

When we turn to the *Categories,* however, all is not plain sailing because it is unclear how the prior and the posterior should be fitted into Aristotle's categorical framework. Thus, in considering the logical status of these terms, we are faced with an initial problem that has not been resolved but merely avoided by giving them the traditional tag of 'Postpraedicamenta.' This is rather like Molière's 'virtus dormitiva' in that it involves the delightful trick of turning one's problems into solutions formulated in suitably obscure phrases.[10] Briefly stated, the problem is that we do not find "the prior and the posterior" listed under any of Aristotle's categories, even though these latter purport to cover all the genera of being. The most natural place to look for them, of course, would be under the category of relatives, since they are clearly correlative terms. But the only trace of them that we find under this category is a single example subsequently used to illustrate a distinct meaning of the prior and the posterior, which itself seems to be tacked on as if it were an afterthought. One might be tempted to resolve the difficulty by lumping the prior and the posterior together with unity and being under the rubric of the so-called transcendentals. The fact that all these terms cross categorical lines makes such a solution initially attractive and I am very tempted by it.[11] But attempts to find in 'prior' and 'posterior' the logical behavior of transcendentals run up against certain inconsistencies in Aristotle's treatment of the multiple senses of these terms. For example, he seems to change his mind about the central or focal meaning of the prior and the posterior, whereas we do not find similar dithering in the case of unity or being.[12]

By contrast, John Duns Scotus shows no hesitation in placing the prior and the posterior under the same rubric as being and unity, since all of them conform to his broad definition of a transcendental as whatever cannot be contained under any genus or category.[13] It should be noted, however, that Scotus is consciously going beyond the traditional conception that required a transcendental to be coextensive or convertible with being. Thus the usual list given contained just six *transcendentia;* namely, *ens, res, aliquid, unum, verum, bonum;*[14] whereas Duns Scotus extended it to include such attributes of being as prior and posterior, act and potency. He makes a general distinction, of course, between such disjunctive transcendentals and those that are correlative with being. Within the former group he also distinguishes between those that are primarily correlatives, like prior and posterior, and those that are either materially or formally contradictories. Thus, according to Scotus, the logical status of prior and posterior is that of transcendentals that are correlative disjunctions. It remains to be seen whether this corresponds with Aristotle's position.

Scotus treats the order of priority and posteriority as coextensive with being (in disjunction) and as an essential order based on the nature of the beings in question.[15] With reference to this, he introduces a further distinction between (i) the order of eminence and (ii) the order of dependence and uses this distinction for interpreting Aristotle's senses of priority. If the essence of something is more perfect and more noble than that of another, it will be prior to it according to the order of eminence.[16] Scotus thinks that this is the kind of priority Aristotle has in mind at *Metaphysics* Theta, where he argues that act is prior to potency according to substance and form. Similarly, Scotus identifies his second kind of priority according to the order of dependence with the sense which Aristotle attributes to Plato in *Metaphysics* Delta; i.e. something is prior according to nature and essence when it can exist without the posterior, while the reverse is not true.[17] While Scotus notes that this might also be described as priority according to substance and species, he thinks it is more precise to describe it as priority according to dependence.

Now such an overlapping of meanings contains the seeds of a problem for the interpretation of Aristotle to which Scotus does not advert, since he is more intent on using the logic of transcendentals for his own natural theology. Historically, in fact, it may have been just such a preoccupation that diverted the attention of commentators away from the original meanings of the prior and the posterior according to Plato and Aristotle. For instance, Scotus and others were intent on proving the *existence* of a Primary Being on whom the existence of all created things depends. But it is not at all obvious that Plato and Aristotle were concerned with the question of existence when they talk about beings that are prior and posterior to one another. Indeed, if we use the *Topics* as a guide to Academic practice, it seems that the prior and the posterior were treated as general attributes of being, at least for the purpose of dialectical discussions. In Book V (ch. 4), for instance, Aristotle includes the prior and the posterior among the "commonplaces" (τόποι) used to establish whether or not certain predicated attributes are properties (ἴσια). In typical dialectical fashion, it can be used either constructively or destructively, depending on which way one wants to make the argument. As part of a destructive argument (ἀνασκευάζοντα), one would try to show that the alleged property cannot possibly belong simultaneously (ἅμα) but must belong as something either posterior or prior (ἢ ὕστερον ἢ πρότερον) to that to which the name of the property belongs; cf. *Top.* 133a12–18. For instance, 'walking through the market-place' is not a property of 'man' because it is not always simultaneous with that subject and may be either prior or posterior to it. By contrast, 'animal receptive of knowledge' must always belong simultaneously with 'man' and is therefore a property, since it is neither a differentia nor a definition. Thus, to make a constructive argument (κατασκευάζοντα), one has to show that the alleged property must always belong simultaneously (ἅμα ἐξ ἀνάγκης ἀεὶ ὑπάρχει) with the subject named, while not being either its definition or differentia; cf. *Top.* 133a18–24.

A few important points emerge from this brief *topos.* First, it is noteworthy that the prior and the posterior are not being contrasted with each other (as we might expect) but that both are set in opposition to what is simultaneous. We will find a similar contrast in the *Categories,* where only the prior and the simultaneous are mentioned. I think that such a contrast must reflect the earlier dialectical usage of the Academy, since Aristotle defines his own views in the *Metaphysics* much more in terms of the contrast between the prior and the posterior. Second, in view of this *topos,* it makes perfect sense for him to identify the latter pair as part of the subject matter of dialectic; cf. *Met.* B1, 995b25. But the context for that identification suggests that as disjuncts they are also general attributes of being, just like same and different, like and unlike, and other such opposites.[18] Yet this would mean that all beings are hierarchically ordered with respect to each other and this seems very strange to our modern eyes. It is not so implausible as an Aristotelian view, however, if we consider his categories as a schema for such a hierarchy. As indirect evidence for this, we should note Aristotle's explicit denial that primary substances are hierachically ordered *with respect to each other;* cf. *Cat.* 2b26–28.[19] Perhaps this may be taken to imply that the other categories are so ordered with reference to each other.[20]

In the course of this monograph but especially in the final chapter, I shall be reviewing many passages that show the influence of hierarchical thinking in Aristotle's philosophy. I am hoping to convince the modern reader of something that medieval commentators accepted without question but for different reasons. What I am trying to get at is the original set of problems and influences that provoked Aristotle into elaborating upon the many different "ways" of priority, alongside the multiplicity of senses for being. In case one should be tempted to neglect the former in deference to the latter, we have his own testimony as to the importance of priority for understanding being. For instance, when he reviews the opinions of the natural philosophers about substance or being, he upbraids them for not clarifying priority and posteriority among the four elements because he thinks that this makes all the difference.[21] Of course, he is concerned there with a particular kind of ordering of the elements with respect to generation but the general point should not be ignored. I hope to present ample evidence that the ordering of all beings in terms of some central kinds of priority is a crucial part of Aristotle's philosophical enterprise.[22]

1

Platonic Background of the *Topics*

IT IS GENERALLY RECOGNIZED THAT THE *TOPICS* IS AN EARLY WORK OF
Aristotle's and that it may be treated as a primer of dialectical practice
within the Academy.[1] Therefore, if we find some statements that do not reflect mature Aristotelian views, we should not be too surprised because that
is consistent with the character of dialectic as he conceives of it. On the
other hand, if he accepts without question a view of essence or substance di-
ametrically opposed to his later view, we should at least be curious and perhaps puzzled about this. This happens in Book VI, for instance, where
Aristotle outlines different ways of refuting or rejecting definitions proposed by one's opponent within the framework of a dialectical joust. In
keeping with that purpose, he gives a number of ways in which one might
overthrow such proposed definitions: (i) One could show that the description cannot be applied to the subject named; for instance, that the proposed
definition (ὁρισμός) of man does not apply to everything called a man. (ii)
One might also show that, although the definiendum has a genus, your opponent has neglected to put it into any genus or has not placed it in the
proper genus (τὸ οἰκεῖου γένος). This would destroy his proposed definition because the definiendum must be placed in its proper genus with its appropriate differentiae if there is to be a genuine definition, especially since
the genus is generally taken to indicate the substance of the definiendum
(τὴν τοῦ ὁριζομένου οὐσίαν). Furthermore, (iii) one could overturn a proposed definition by showing that the description is not peculiar to the
definiendum, given that this is at least a necessary condition for a correct
definition. Finally, (iv) even if your opponent has satisfied all the foregoing,
he may still have failed to give a definition inasmuch as he has not stated the
essence (τὸ τί ἦν εἶναι) of the definiendum.

For the purposes of this monograph, the last way in which a proposed definition can fail turns out to be of most interest. We find it taken up again
and elucidated in the fourth chapter (of Book VI) where Aristotle suggests
some rules for determining whether or not one's opponent has stated and
defined the essence of the definiendum:

First of all, see if he has failed to make the definition through terms that are prior and more intelligible. For the reason why the definition is rendered is to make known the term stated, and we make things known by taking not any random terms, but such as are prior and more intelligible, as is done in demonstrations (for so it is with all teaching and learning); accordingly, it is clear that a man who does not define through terms of this kind has not defined at all.[2]

The clear message here is that a genuine definition must be framed in terms that are both prior and more intelligible, otherwise the essence of the definiendum will not have been given. Aristotle claims that the basic purpose of definition (i.e. making known the thing in question) cannot be achieved through any chance terms but only through those that are prior and more intelligible. Thus he is assuming without explanation that such terms are essential for making known the essence of the thing to be defined. Yet, when he draws an explicit comparison with the procedure in demonstrations (ἐν ταῖς ἀποδείξεσιν), he gives us a clue as to where an explanation might be found. An additional justification for turning to the *Posterior Analytics* can be found in the echo of its opening line that is here contained in Aristotle's parenthetical remark about "all teaching and learning" (πᾶσα διδασκαλία καὶ μάθησις).

An Important Distinction in the *Posterior Analytics*

Since I am mainly seeking clarification for a passage from the *Topics,* I do not propose to say much here about the general project of the *Posterior Analytics*. For my purposes it is more enlightening to focus upon the statement in Book I (ch. 2) where Aristotle insists that demonstrative knowledge must proceed from premises that are true (ἀληθῶν), primary (πρώτων), immediate (ἀμέσων), more intelligible than and prior to (γνωριμωτέρων καὶ προτέρων) the conclusion in respect to which they are causes (αἰτίων); cf. 71b20–23.[3] He goes on to say that demonstrative knowledge will only be possible when all of these conditions are fulfilled and when, as a result, the starting points (αἱ ἀρχαί) are appropriate to the demonstrandum. Taking each one of the conditions in turn, he briefly explains its role in demonstration. As Barnes[4] points out in his commentary, these conditions fall roughly into two groups that contain absolute and relative features, respectively. While this helps us to understand why "priority" seems to be duplicated in the list, we still need to elucidate the precise relationship between its absolute and relative senses. Aristotle appears to equate premises that are primary in a simple sense with those that are indemonstrable (ἀναποδείκτων) and, therefore, immediate. For instance, he argues that if these premises are not primary and nondemonstrable then we must have knowledge of them through demonstration. But any such demonstration would require other premises that are themselves either primary and indemonstrable or secondary and demonstrable. Since the latter option would lead to an infinite regress, Aristotle insists there must be some premises that are simply prior and indemonstrable if genuine demonstration is to be possible. But, since such demonstration *is* possible, it follows that there are immediate premises that have no other premises prior to them; cf. 72a6–8. Thus, judging by the course of this argument, it would appear that the simple (or unqualified) sense of priority applies to premises (rather than terms) that are immediate and indemonstrable.[5]

By comparison, it would seem that priority in the relative sense may be applicable to terms as well as to premises. Aristotle consistently links relative priority with what is more familiar (γνωριμώτερον) and finds it necessary to distinguish two meanings of these concepts:

There are two senses in which things are prior and more knowable. That which is prior in nature is not the same as that which is prior in relation to us, and that which is (naturally) more knowable is not the same as that which is more knowable by us. By "prior" or "more knowable" in relation to us I mean that which is nearer our perception, and by "prior" or "more knowable" in the absolute sense I mean that which is further from it. The most universal concepts are furthest from our perception, and particulars are nearest to it; and these are opposite to one another.[6]

Though the context for this passage is not my concern here, I think it may be helpful to notice some things about the way in which the above distinction is elaborated upon by Aristotle. First, it is obvious from the Greek that πρότερον and γνωριμώτερον are comparatives frequently used in conjunction to describe related characteristics of premises and their terms. Second, having conjoined these characteristics in such a consistent fashion, he also makes the same distinction for both between their two different senses; i.e. what is prior and better known by nature (τῇ φύσει) is distinguished from what is prior and better known to us (πρὸς ἡμᾶς). Yet, I have doubts about Tredennick's conjecture that "naturally" should be supplied from the context as the implicit qualifier of the first γνωριμώτερον; cf. *An. Pst.* 72a1. The very fact that Aristotle leaves it without qualification suggests that ἁπλῶς would be a more appropriate epithet.[7] Third, the close link between priority and greater intelligibility is reinforced when he goes on to explain that things closer to perception (τὰ ἐγγύτερον τῆς αἰσθήσεως) are both prior and more intelligible in relation to us. By contrast, those things that are further from perception (τὰ πορρώτερον) are both prior and more intelligible in an absolute sense (ἁπλῶς). Within the context, I think we can confidently equate this sense with priority by nature (τῇ φύσει).

Thus we can infer from what Aristotle says about the most universal things (τὰ καθόλου μάλιστα) being most remote from sensation that he would hold them to be more intelligible absolutely and prior by nature. On the other hand, particular things (τὰ καθ' ἕκαστα) are closest to perception and, presumably, are prior and more familiar in relation to us.[8] Such a contrast between universals and particulars with respect to natural priority should immediately strike us as odd, since it appears to reverse what is generally accepted to be the order of reality according to Aristotle.[9] Another oddity is the apparent move from priority as a characteristic of premises to greater priority and intelligibility as characteristics of terms. Perhaps this move has something to do with the overlapping senses of priority in the original list of six characteristics Aristotle associates with the premises of a demonstrative syllogism. For instance, what is prior in an absolute sense seems to be a whole premise only, whereas the relative sense may also refer to the terms that constitute such a premise and that could have greater priority either in relation to us or by nature. If universal terms are prior by nature, as the passage suggests, they would satisfy the logical conditions applicable to premises in a demonstrative syllogism of the paradigmatic sort; i.e. first figure (Barbara).

I think that further light can be thrown on the priority condition for demonstrative premises when we look at another passage from *Posterior Analytics* A3, where Aristotle refutes what he regards as two false views about first principles. According to him, the necessity of knowing the primary truths (τὰ πρῶτα) has led some people to think that there is no knowledge (ἐπιστήμη), while others admit the possibility of knowledge but think that everything is demonstrable. Aristotle responds that neither view is true nor logically necessary and he refutes each of them in turn. Even though he does not identify the authors of these views, he gives us enough information to reconstruct their arguments. The first group of people, who claim that there is no knowing whatsoever, appear to give an argument in the form of a dilemma: (i) either there is an infinite regress of premises with no absolute firsts (ii) or if there are firsts these cannot be known, since they cannot be demonstrated. The basic assumption in the argument is that demonstration is the only form of knowledge, and as a result of the dilemma, it concludes that knowledge is impossible. I find the first horn to be of greatest interest because it depends on the claim that we cannot know posterior things (τὰ ὕστερα) through prior things (τὰ πρότερα) that are not simple firsts (πρῶτα); cf. *An. Pst.* 72b9–10. Here we see the distinction between relative and absolute priority doing some important work, since Aristotle agrees that there will be an infinite regress if none of the things that are relatively prior can be identified as something absolutely prior.[10] On the other hand (the argument continues with the second horn), if there is a stand (ἵσταται) and there are first principles (ἀρχαί), these will be unknowable because they cannot be demonstrated; cf. *An. Pst.* 72b11–13. Thus, if it is not possible to know the primary things (τὰ πρῶτα), neither can the inferences drawn from them be known in the simple or strict sense (ἁπλῶς οὐδε κυρίως) but only hypothetically (ἐξ ὑποθέσεως). Even if we accept the conjecture about Antisthenes being the author of this dilemma, we must assume from the language that he is drawing upon the example of mathematics and its hypothetical starting points. In the *Republic* Plato had also noted this paradoxical feature of the paradigm science and, by way of solution, proposed that it be grounded in the highest science of dialectic. But so far as we can tell from the *Posterior Analytics,* Aristotle has rejected such a "mistress science" of reality and thus he offers his own resolution of the dilemma by challenging the fundamental assumption upon which it is based.

"We say," he begins, "that not all science is demonstrative but that knowledge of immediate things is indemonstrable."[11] Aristotle insists it is obvious that this must be the case and goes on to offer an argument that implicitly depends upon the distinction between priority in the relative and absolute senses. Since it is necessary to know the prior things (τὰ πρότερα) from which the demonstration is made and since this potential regress stops at the immediate things (τὰ ἄμεσα), he argues that these latter must be indemonstrable. Yet Aristotle is clearly aware that his solution to the dilemma is incomplete as it stands because the question about how these absolutely first things are known remains unanswered. Clarifying his position, therefore, he adds that there is not only (demonstrative) science but also "some principle of science by which we become familiar with the definitions."[12] Aristotle does not explain further but I think that "principle of science" must be a reference to *nous,* which is denoted elsewhere by precisely the same phrase.[13] In fact, in a subsequent chapter (A 23) that rejects the possibility of an infinite regress in demonstration, we get the following suggestive parallel: just as an immediate premise (πρότασις ἄμεσος) is the unit in a syllogism, so *nous* is the unit in demonstrative science; cf. *An. Pst.* 85a1–2. Within the context of Aristotle's discussion, what this parallel suggests to me is that *nous* is the indivisible unit of measure for demonstration in the sense that it terminates any regress by being the simple principle (ἡ ἀρχὴ ἁπλοῦν) that grasps the immediate premise or the crucial middle term.

While the first group is thus refuted by the argument that there is something which is prior in an absolute sense, the claims of the second group are met with the distinction between two different senses of relative priority:

> And that it is impossible to demonstrate *simpliciter* circularly is clear, if demonstration must depend on what is prior and more familiar; for it is impossible for the same things at the same time to be prior and posterior to the same things—unless one is so in the other fashion (i.e. one in relation to us, the other *simpliciter*), which fashion induction makes familiar. But if so, knowing *simpliciter* will not have been properly defined, but will be twofold. Or is the other demonstration not <demonstration> *simpliciter* in that it comes about from what is more familiar *to us*? [14]

Briefly put, the position of the second group (sometimes conjectured to be Xenocrates and his followers) is that all knowledge is demonstrative and that everything may be demonstrated, since circular or reciprocal proofs are acceptable. In his attempted refutation, Aristotle argues that circular proof cannot be demonstration in the strict sense (ἁπλῶς), since such a demonstration must come from premises that are both prior (προτέρων) and more intelligible (γνωριμωτέρων). Here he is obviously referring back to some of the essential conditions for demonstrative premises, which he has explained and justified in the previous passage that we examined. Appealing to the principle of contradiction, Aristotle insists that it is impossible for the same things to be simultaneously prior and posterior (ἅμα πρότερα καὶ ὕστερα) to the same things in the same respect. He concedes, of course, that this is possible in different respects, such as when something is prior to us (πρὸς ἡμᾶς) but posterior in an absolute sense (ἁπλῶς).

When he adds that this difference is made familiar by induction (ἐπαγωγὴ), I presume that Aristotle has in mind something similar to the previous passage, where he says that particulars are prior to us because they are closer to sensation whereas universals are prior absolutely, since they are most distant from sense perception. Thus the distinction between different senses of priority would become obvious through the 'way' from the particular to the universal, which is called "induction." Now there are clear hints in the above passage that Aristotle considers the second group of thinkers to be trading upon these ambiguities in 'priority' so as to make their case for circular proof. If they are including induction as a kind of demonstration then his response is that knowing in the strict sense (ἁπλῶς) has not been well defined, since it would now have two senses. But even if one were to concede that the other kind of showing forth (ἡ ἑτέρα ἀπόδειξις), which begins from things more familiar to us (ἐκ τῶν ἡμῖν γνωριμωτέρων), is a sort of proof, this does not make it demonstration in the strict sense. Hence we can see that the distinction between different senses of priority and intelligibility helps Aristotle here in specifying his epistemological position vis-à-vis contemporary thinkers who held competing views on scientific knowledge. Yet, it is possible that he was initially indebted to Plato for the distinction between the way from the principles (ἀπὸ τῶν ἀρχῶν) and the way to the principles (ἐπὶ τὰς ἀρχάς); cf. *EN* 1, iv, 1095a30–b3.[15] Perhaps he is simply developing that distinction when he claims that there are two ways in which things can be prior and more intelligible.[16]

Platonic Sources for the Distinction

Let us leave this digression into the *Posterior Analytics* and return to the original task of clarifying a puzzling passage in the *Topics*. The conclusion of the passage quoted above (VI, 4, 141a26–32) is that whoever does not frame his definition in terms that are prior and more intelligible has not given a definition at all. If this were not the case, the argument goes on, there would be many definitions of the same thing. Suppose that someone gives a definition of X, while someone else gives another definition of X in terms that are prior and more intelligible. In that case both would have given definitions of the same thing, even though it is clear (according to generally accepted principles) that the latter has given the better definition. But such a state of affair is unacceptable because each thing is thought to have a single essence that makes it be just what it is.[17] If there were a number of different definitions of the same thing X, this would lead to the impossible result that X has many different essences. Therefore, the argument concludes, it is obvious that whoever has not framed his definition by means of prior and more intelligible terms (διὰ προτέρων καὶ γνωριμωτέρων) has not really given a definition.

If we did not read any further into the passage, we might think that Aristotle is ignoring the distinction between different senses in which things can be called 'prior' and 'more intelligible.' But it is precisely at this point in the argument that he introduces the same distinction:

> That the definition has not been stated in more intelligible terms can be taken in two senses, namely, that it is composed either of terms which are less intelligible absolutely or of terms which are less intelligible to us; for both meanings are possible. Thus absolutely the prior is more intelligible than the posterior; for example, a point is more intelligible than a line, a line than a plane, a plane

than a solid; just as also a unit is more intelligible than a number, since it is prior to and the starting-point of all number. Similarly a letter is more intelligible than a syllable. To us, however, the converse sometimes happens; for a solid falls most under our perception, and a plane more than a line, a line more than a point. For most people recognise such things as solids and planes before they recognise lines and points; for the former can be grasped by an ordinary understanding, the latter only by one which is accurate and superior.[18]

What is of great interest about this passage is that it prompts us to ask whether Aristotle's own metaphysical stance here is not characteristically Platonic.[19] Before addressing these general issues, however, let us take a closer look at the passage itself. Just as in the parallel passage from the *Posterior Analytics,* Aristotle draws a general distinction between what is more intelligible absolutely (ἁπλῶς) and what is more intelligible to us (πρὸς ἡμᾶς). At first sight it would appear that priority has been dropped from the distinction but a more careful scrutiny shows that this is not the case. The notion of priority, in fact, serves as an objective point of reference in the explanation of what it means to say that something is "more intelligible" in an absolute sense. When we look at the examples that are used in this explanation, it becomes more obvious that a certain schema of priority is already present as a background assumption. For instance, the point is said to be more intelligible in an absolute sense than the line because it is prior to it. Similarly, within the same schema of priority, a line is held to be more intelligible than a plane, while a plane is in turn more intelligible than a solid. We are not told explicitly what kind of priority Aristotle has in mind but we may hazard a guess from the guiding example in the passage. The unit is said to be more intelligible than number because it is prior to (πρότερον) and the principle of (ἀρχή) all number. From such an explanation one can safely conjecture that natural priority is involved and this is confirmed by the close link between this kind of priority and greater intelligibility in an absolute sense.[20] Since the relationship between unit and number is made the paradigm for such priority, we can also apply the explanation generally to the other parallel examples. Thus we can say that the point is more intelligible than the line, and the line more so than the plane, and the plane more so than the solid, since each is a principle of the other and hence prior to it by nature.

In fact, what is being used here by Aristotle for the purposes of illustration is recognizable as an Academic[21] schema of natural priority according to which the plane, for instance, is prior to the solid because planes both limit and mark off a body as a definite thing. Hence (the argument goes), when these limits are destroyed, the whole body is also destroyed—ὧν ἀναιρουμένων ἀναιρεῖται τὸ ὅλον—cf. *Met.* 1017b18–19. When Aristotle is listing the various meanings of 'substance' (οὐσία) at *Metaphysics* Delta 8, he uses this formulaic phrase together with the same examples to characterize this way of thinking about substance. Furthermore, at Beta 5 (1002a4–12), he reports a similar criterion as guiding some unnamed thinkers to the conclusion that the body (τὸ σῶμα) is less substantial (ἧττον οὐσία) than the planes and lines that limit and define it.[22] The basic reason given for this conclusion is that these defining boundaries "are thought to be capable of existing without body, whereas the body cannot exist without them."[23] Clearly, this passage presents us with a concrete application of the formula contained in the Delta passage. In fact, both passages may be taken as parallel accounts of the same way of thinking about substance, which was probably influential within the Academy.[24] When pursued to its logical conclusion, Aristotle claims, this line of thinking yields the result that numbers are prior in substance to everything else because they are the defining limits without which other things would not exist.[25]

Now, when we recall that the numerical unit (μονάς) is sometimes described as a point without position,[26] we can recognize the influence of such thinking in the *Topics* passage under scrutiny. It is plausible to see the schema of point, line, plane, and solid as having been ultimately derived from the unit through the addition of a dimension in each case. This appears to be in the background also at *Posterior Analytics* A 27, where Aristotle says that the science of arithmetic is more accurate than and prior to the science of geometry because the former depends upon fewer principles than the latter science, which brings in additional principles. In explaining what he means by "from addition" (ἐκ προσθέσεως), he contrasts the point with the unit as follows: whereas the unit is a substance without position (οὐσία ἄθετος), the point is a substance with position (οὐσία θετός) and hence involves the addition of a dimension within which a point can be located. I find it very significant that Aristotle should use 'substance' terminology here with reference to mathematical objects like the unit and the point, especially within the context of his discussion of the priority and the accuracy of the sciences in relation to each other. What it suggests to me is that the metaphysical framework for such a discussion is still being structured by the Platonic assumption that priority in knowledge also involves ontological priority.[27] If one accepts this assumption, then it follows that the unit is prior in substance to the point, the point to the line, the line to the plane, and the plane to the solid. This constitutes a system of non-reversible ontological dependence, which was probably reflected in the Academic rules for the proper order of mathematical demonstration. Such a system can also be seen to result from an application of the specific criterion for priority "according to nature and substance" (κατὰ φύσιν καὶ οὐσίαν), which Aristotle attributes to Plato by name in *Metaphysics* Delta 11. But I will postpone my discussion of this criterion until chapters 2 and 3, where I will be comparing Aristotle's different treatments of the many senses of priority.

Having established this Academic perspective, I can now bring out some implications hidden in the above passage from the *Topics*. When Aristotle distinguishes between what is more intelligible to us and what is more intelligible absolutely, it is clear from his examples that he has in mind the practice of mathematics within the Academy. He feels compelled to make this distinction because he recognizes that the mathematical sciences require a kind of thinking that is different from the ordinary. Thus, at the end of the passage, he contrasts our ordinary intelligence (τῆς τυχούσης . . . διανοίας) with the precise and extraordinary (ἀκριβοῦς καί περιττῆς) understanding demanded in mathematics. Since our ordinary understanding of things is dominated by sense perception, what is more intelligible to us sometimes happens to be the complete reverse of what is more intelligible by nature, especially in the case of mathematical objects. For instance, as Aristotle points out, the solid (τὸ στερεόν) is most obvious to sense perception, while the plane (τὸ ἐπίπεδον) is more obvious than the line (τῆς γραμμῆς), and the line more so than the point (τοῦ σημείου).

Hence we can see that the order established by perception cuts completely against the order of definition in mathematics. Yet, in spite of this, Aristotle goes on to insist that the mathematical order of definition is "more scientific" (ἐπιστημονικώτερον), and on this basis, he gives the following advice:

Absolutely, therefore, the attempt to come to know what is posterior by means of what is prior is better because such (a way) is more scientific. But yet, for those who are unable to come to know by means of such (prior) things, it may perhaps be necessary that the account be given by means of those things which are familiar to them. Among definitions of this kind are those of a point, a line, and a plane, all of which clarify the prior through the posterior; for they say that a point is the limit of a line, a line that of a plane, a plane that of a solid. However, one must not hide the fact that those who define in this way cannot show the essence of what they define, unless it so happens that the same thing is both more familiar to us and also absolutely. The reason for this is that a correct definition must define a thing through its genus and its differentiae, and these belong to the order of things which are absolutely more familiar than, and prior to, the species. For the genus and the differentia destroy the species, so that these are prior to the species.[28]

The emphatic position of "absolutely" (ἁπλῶς) clearly establishes the point of view from which Aristotle insists that it is "better" (βέλτιον) to try to gain knowledge of posterior things (τὰ ὕστερα) by means of what is prior (διὰ τῶν πρότερον). From what has gone before, we may conjecture that he has in mind the mathematical procedure of defining what is posterior in terms of what is prior by nature, according to the criterion of priority already outlined. Therefore, given the paradigmatic role of mathematics within the Academy, it should not surprise us to find such a procedure being called "more scientific." Still, in contrast to this, there is another approach to definition that Aristotle seems ready to concede as being necessary in the case of people who are not used to acquiring knowledge in the scientific manner. Possibly he has in mind the situation of a learner with an untutored intelligence who is making his first approach to a new subject matter. In such a case it may be necessary, for instance, to describe a figure as "the limit of a solid" (στερεοῦ πέρας), just as Socrates does in the *Meno* (76A) for the benefit of a particularly obdurate student. Our own appreciation of the irony involved in this exchange between Socrates and Meno is further enhanced by the knowledge that such a definition would be treated as unscientific within the Academy.

But the whole passage in the *Meno* (75–77) seems to provide evidence for the existence of an alternative tradition of "concrete" definition among some Presocratic thinkers.[29] This appears to be confirmed by Aristotle in the present passage from the *Topics,* where he gives examples of such alternative definitions for mathematical entities like the solid, the plane, the line, and the point. For instance, we find him giving a 'definition' of the plane as "the limit of a solid" (στερεοῦ . . . πέρας) and this is just one of a series of such definitions proposed by some unnamed thinkers. According to Aristotle, all of these definitions provide examples of defining what is prior in terms of what is posterior.[30]

But he clearly hews the Platonic line when he insists that those people who define in this way cannot show the essence (τὸ τί ἦν εἶναι) of the definiendum, unless it should so happen that the same thing is both more intelligible to us (ἡμῖν . . . γνωριμώτερον) and more intelligible absolutely (ἁπλῶς). In view of what has gone before, I think we may safely conclude that Aristotle does not consider such a coincidence of the two senses of 'more intelligible' to be the usual state of affairs with respect to mathematical entities. Furthermore, in a subsequent passage (142a9–12), he says that what is intelligible absolutely (τὸ ἁπλῶς γνώριμον) is not identical with what is intelligible to everyone (τὸ πᾶσι γνώριμον) but rather with what is intelligible to those who are in a sound state of understanding (τοῖς εὖ διακειμένοις τὴν διάνοιαν). Similarly, he says, what is healthy absolutely (τὸ ἁπλῶς ὑγιεινὸν) is identical with what is healthy for those in sound physical condition. In order to avoid any subjectivist misunderstandings of this whole passage, we must interpret it in the light of a prior discussion (141b34–142a8) emphasizing that a true definition is not given merely in terms more intelligible to any individual, since such terms may change over time according to the state of knowledge of the person involved. At the beginning, for instance, sensible things may be more familiar to him but this is reversed as his knowledge becomes more accurate. Nevertheless, those who claim that a definition must be given in terms that are more familiar to each individual are thereby implying that there are at least two definitions of the same thing. But this yields the absurd conclusion that the same thing has two or more essences. Therefore, the only way to guarantee that the same thing will have one and the same definition is to insist that it be formulated in terms that are more intelligible absolutely.[31]

We can see from this whole discussion that Aristotle does not intend to deny the existence of absolute standards of health and intelligibility. In fact, he is clearly presupposing such standards when he talks about people who are in a sound state of physical or intellectual health. The point is that only a few people ever come close to reaching these standards, and hence, they are the best available measures of what is healthy or more intelligible in an absolute sense. He implicitly suggests that some process of education is usually necessary to bring what is more intelligible to us into line with what is more intelligible by nature. This is the case especially for exact sciences like mathematics, which require a mode of thought that is different from the ordinary and it also seems to be true of the Platonic science of dialectic, so far as we can judge from the above passage where Aristotle explains that a good definition of a thing must be framed in terms of its genus and proper differentiae. Obviously, these conditions for correct definition are part of the legacy of Plato, since they are intimately related to the method of division in dialectic.

This is implicitly confirmed by Aristotle himself in this *Topics* passage when he goes on to explain why the genus and the differentiae are absolutely prior to and more intelligible than the species. In explaining why they are prior, he appeals to what is recognizable as a Platonic criterion; i.e. that the removal of the genus or differentiae can destroy (συναναιρεῖ) the species and hence they are prior to it.[32] In other words, the species cannot exist without the genus and the differentiae; whereas the reverse is not the case. This may be taken as a specific application of the general criterion for priority with respect to substance and nature, which Aristotle attributes to Plato elsewhere. Hence, from the point of view being adopted here, there is no doubt the genus is naturally prior to the species. Indeed, the Platonic perspective throws more light on Aristotle's emphatic statement that the essence (τὸ τί ἦν εἶναι) can be made known only through terms that are prior and more intelligible in the absolute sense. It is clear how the definition of a species by means of its genus and appropriate differentiae satisfies this condition, since they are prior to, and more intelligible than, the species according to the relevant Platonic criterion. Another reason for this being the correct mode of definition has already been given at the beginning of Book VI, where Aristotle says that the genus seems to indicate the substance of the definiendum.[33] Hence, in order to give a true definition of any species, it is crucial to find its proper genus. The failure to give such a definition can be detected through the so-called commonplace (τόπος) dealing with the prior and the more intelligible; cf. *Top.* 142b20–22.

Yet, in spite of the dialectical character of this whole passage from the *Topics,* Aristotle's espousal of a Platonic view on correct definition should raise some question in our minds about his ontological stance. There is a prima facie case for saying that he uncritically adopts some fundamental elements of Plato's ontology.[34] For instance, Aristotle seems to accept without reservation that the genus is naturally prior to, and more intelligible than, the species in an absolute sense. But surely this conflicts with what he says elsewhere[35] about the universal genus being less substantial (and hence posterior by nature) than the particular species. From my perspective, however, what is most interesting about this passage is Aristotle's apparent acceptance of the natural priority of point to line to plane to solid. This would suggest that, at a certain point in his philosophical development, he accepted the mathematical ontology of the Platonists because it fitted the "more scientific" procedure of definition. As evidence for this, we might count his refusal to accept that any alternate definitions could show the essence (τὸ τί ἦν εἶναι) of the definiendum. But, on the other hand, we should perhaps note that essence is the most *logical* of Aristotle's four causes.[36] Thus he need not be making a specific *ontological* commitment when he insists that the essence of a definiendum can be given only by a definition that is formally correct; i.e. with proper genus and appropriate differentiae. In order to illustrate such correct definitions, he might be simply drawing upon the standard examples of mathematical definition within the Academy, without accepting the concomitant ontological framework. But such a difficult balancing act Aristotle only perfects later (if at all) in *Metaphysics* Mu, and there is no evidence in the *Topics* that he has distinguished between logical and ontological implications. Furthermore, the present passage contains no hint that he is trying to distance himself from Platonism in mathematics.

What is clear from this passage, however, is that the question about priority is a central one in the Platonic tradition that Aristotle inherited. Therefore, in developing his own problematic, he is likely to rethink this question. My proposal in this monograph is that a revealing way to study this problem-situation would be to compare and contrast a number of the different elaborations on the many senses of priority we find throughout the Aristotelian corpus. In fact, I find this more revealing in certain respects than his thesis about the many senses of being, even though there is a close connection between the two. Within the compass of a short monograph, however, I can only cover this ground with reference to some particular aspects of Aristotle's thought and I have already made a start with the epistemological distinction between what is prior to us and what is prior absolutely or by nature.

Conclusion

In this chapter I have tried to locate within the epistemological contexts of the *Topics* and the *Posterior Analytics* what I take to be an early use by Aristotle of the distinction between different senses of priority so as to resolve inherited problems. By means of such an approach, I hope to promote a fresh understanding of Aristotle's philosophical problem-situation by unearthing its Platonic background with reference to the topic of priority. There is every reason to believe that Plato attached great importance to priority in his own thinking, since a superficial survey of the dialogues yields at least five different senses that have philosophical significance.[37] Thus it should be quite revealing to examine how Aristotle develops his own philosophical views with reference to this preestablished matrix of meanings. Even though I am confining myself of necessity to his logical and metaphysical works in which priority seems to play a greater role, there is no reason why this line of inquiry could not be pursued also for his ethical and physical works.

2

The Senses of Priority in the *Categories*

I PROPOSE TO BEGIN WITH A SURVEY OF THE MANY SENSES OF PRIORITY LISTED in the *Categories,* in view of the consensus among modern scholars about it being one of Aristotle's early works.[1] Even though the treatment of priority given here is rather sketchy and clearly different[2] from that contained in *Metaphysics* Delta, it is still of great interest because it shows how some Platonic modes of thought remained influential for Aristotle. Perhaps the most surprising aspect of this particular treatment, however, is that it does not appear to reflect the priorities among substances and attributes that are established in the earlier parts of the *Categories.*[3] It seems to me rather strange that not a single example of priority is drawn from the relationship between the different categories of predication.[4] He could have referred back to *Categories* 5, for instance, where the species (τὸ εἶδος) is held to be prior to the genus (τὸ γένος) because it would be more intelligible and more appropriate (γνωριμώτερον καὶ οἰκειότερον) as an answer to the 'what is it?' (τί ἐστι;) question about a primary substance. From such an explanation it is clear that this sense of priority is closely related to greater intelligibility, but contrary to what is said in the *Topics,* the species is now declared to be more intelligible than the genus with reference to definition.

While this represents a definite shift in this meaning of priority, there is no trace of it in the schematic account of priority in *Categories* 12. Indeed, any such shift seems to be directly negated in the subsequent chapter when Aristotle declares that genera are always prior to species; cf. *Cat.* 15a4–5. Furthermore, there is no trace of the distinction between primary and secondary substance that is made in chapter 5 as follows:

A substance—that which is called a substance most strictly (κυριώτατα), primarily (πρώτως), and most of all (μάλιστα)—is that which is neither said of a subject nor in a subject, e.g. the individual man or the individual horse. The species in which the things primarily called substances are, are called secondary substances, as also are the genera of these species (τὰ τῶν εἰδῶν τούτων γένη). For example, the individual man belongs in a species, man, and animal is a genus of the species; so these—both man and animal—are called secondary substances.[5]

This passage clearly states an important relationship of priority with respect to substance between the individual thing and the species and/or genus that is used to describe it.[6] But this example of priority does not seem to be noted in chapters 12 and 13, where we get the distinct impression that universals are held to be more substantial than particulars. Given such apparent inconsistencies, it should be obvious that a fresh scrutiny of the different senses of priority listed in the *Categories* is necessary.[7] My procedure will be as follows: First, I will give a translation of the relevant text, and then, I will discuss, in turn, each of the corresponding meanings of priority and simultaneity.

Translation of *Categories* 12 and 13[8]

One thing is called prior to another in four ways. First and most strictly, with respect to time, as when one thing is called older and more ancient than another; for it is because the time is longer that it is called both older and more ancient. Second, what does not reciprocate as to implication of being (is called prior). For example, one is prior to two because if there are two it follows at once that there is one; whereas if there is one there are not necessarily two. Thus the implication of being for the other does not hold reciprocally from the one; and that from which the implication of being does not hold reciprocally is thought to be prior. Third, a thing is called prior with respect to some order, as with sciences and speeches. Thus in the demonstrative sciences there is a prior and posterior in order, since the elements are prior in order to the propositions,[9] and in grammar the letters (of the alphabet) are prior to the syllables. And likewise with speeches, since the introduction is prior in order to the exposition. Further, besides the ways mentioned, what is better and more valued is thought to be prior by nature. Ordinary men, too, usually speak of those whom they honor more or love more as being prior. But this way of priority is just about the furthest removed from the other ways.[10]

Therefore these ways of speaking about the prior are almost as many as there are. Besides those mentioned, however, it would seem that there is another way (of speaking) of priority. For, among the things that reciprocate as to implication of being, that which is in any way the cause of another's being may reasonably be called prior by nature. But that there are some such cases is obvious. For being a man reciprocates as to implication of being with the true statement about him; e.g. if there is a man then there is a true statement by which we say that there is a man. Reciprocally, if the statement is true by which we say that there is a man then there is a man. But, whereas the true statement is in no way the cause of the thing's being, still the thing appears to be somehow the cause of the statement's being true. For it is on account of the thing being or not being that the statement is either true or false.

So there are five ways in which one thing may be called prior to another.

Those things are called simultaneous, without qualification and in the strictest sense, whose coming into being is at the same time, because neither one of them is earlier nor later.[11] So these are called simultaneous with respect to time. But those things are (called) simultaneous by nature that reciprocate as to implication of being, while one of them is not in any way the cause of being with respect to the other; just as in the case of the double and the half. For, although these reciprocate because if there is a double then there is also a half and if there is a half then there is also a double, still neither of them is a cause of being with respect to the other.

Also the coordinate divisions from the same genus are called simultaneous by nature. Those things that result from the same division are said to be coordinated with each other; for example, the winged (is coordinated) with the footed and with the aquatic. For these beings are contradistinguished from each other out of the same genus, since 'animal' is divided into these; i.e. into the winged and the footed and the aquatic. And none of these is either prior or posterior but rather such (divisions) are thought to be simultaneous by nature. [However, one could divide again into species each of such divisions; i.e. the footed and the winged and the aquatic.][12] Therefore, these will be simultaneous by nature inasmuch as they come from the same genus in the course of the same division. Yet the genera are always prior to the species because they do not reciprocate as to implication of being. For there to be an aquatic, for example, there must be an animal but for there to be an animal it is not necessary for it to be aquatic.

Hence, those things are said to be simultaneous by nature (*a*) that reciprocate as to implication of being, while not being in any way the cause of being with respect to one another, and (*b*) those things that are coordinate divisions from the same genus. On the other hand, those things are said to be simultaneous without qualification whose coming into being is at the same time.

Priority and Simultaneity in Time

The account in *Categories* 12 begins by stating that one thing is called prior to another in four ways (τετραχῶς), but it ends, rather surprisingly, with the conclusion that there are five ways (κατὰ πέντε τρόπους). Perhaps this is an afterthought, since the fifth way turns out to be closely related to one of the other senses. In spite of such an inherent connection, however, it is unequivocally presented as a separate sense of priority; cf. *Cat.*14b1–11. Thus, as we go through the different senses of priority that are listed, we shall find that the whole account is rather loosely organized.[13] The first sense of 'priority' that is mentioned is priority with respect to time (κατὰ τὸν χρόνον) and this is said to be the principal or strictest (κυριώτατα)[14] meaning; cf. *Cat.*14a27. The example given for this kind of priority is the case where one thing is called older or more ancient than another. In this case, Aristotle explains, one thing is called older "on account of the time being longer."[15] He appears to neglect the fact that, in the case of future time, what is prior from our present point of view is the event that is the smallest distance in time from us. The absence of this point tends to suggest that this account of priority in time antedates the one contained in *Metaphysics* Delta 11.[16]

To find the meaning that is contrary to priority in time, we must turn to *Categories* 13, which gives an account of the different senses in which things are said to be simultaneous. Just as in the previous discussion, pride of place is given to time. According to Aristotle's account, those things that come into being at the same time are called simultaneous in the absolute (ἁπλῶς) or strictest (κυριώτατα) sense. The reason why these things are said to be simultaneous with respect to time (κατὰ τὸν χρόνον) is simply that none of them comes into being before or after (πρότερον ... ὕστερον) the rest. From this explanation I think it is quite clear that the principal meaning of simultaneity both corresponds to, and is dependent upon, the principal meaning of priority in *Categories* 12.[17] Ultimately, of course, Aristotle is appealing to a feature of the Greek language itself when he says that things are "called" (λέγεται) prior or simultaneous most strictly and without qualification, when one is talking about their temporal relationship to one another. But, in both accounts, this meaning is treated as unproblematic perhaps because it is obvious to everyone in the language community who shares the same experience of time. We find no hint of the complexity that Aristotle must introduce into his account of temporal priority within a teleological framework. But let me postpone discussion of this to a later chapter.[18]

Priority and Simultaneity in Being

For the purposes of this monograph, I am more interested in the second sense of priority listed in *Categories* 12; i.e. the priority of what does not reciprocate as to the implication of being.[19] It seems to me that the purpose of this convoluted and rather formulaic phrase is to refer to systems of nonreversible dependency like numbering.[20] By way of illustrating this kind of priority, Aristotle cites the relation between one and two in the number system. If it is the case that there are two things, then it follows immediately (ἀκολουθεῖ εὐθὺς) that there is one; yet the reverse is not the case, for there may be one thing without it being necessary that there are two. Thus, as Aristotle puts it, "the implication of being for the other does not hold reciprocally from the one."[21] If we want to cash out this formula as a test for priority, we might proceed as follows: Take the number two in isolation and ask what it implies. The answer seems to be that its very being implies a principle of numbering (i.e. the one) but it does not imply any of the subsequent numbers. Hence, according to such a criterion of priority, two is prior to three but posterior to one. But I think that this test case can also be applied in a less obvious example than the number system. In plane geometry, for instance, we may take the notion of a line and ask about its implications with respect to being. Quite clearly, a line implies the existence of points that serve as its limits or mark out its divisions. But a point does not reciprocally imply the existence of a line, since points may be taken in isolation as simply marking positions. Therefore, a point is prior to a line with respect to implication of being. Similarly, by the same criterion, a line can be seen to be prior to a plane and a plane to a solid. In this way we can reproduce the system of priority that we have already seen to be associated with another Platonic criterion of ontological dependency.

In the next chapter I will try to show that this overlapping of schemata is no coincidence, but for the moment, let me simply note a further application of the criterion of nonreciprocation in *Categories* 13. There Aristotle makes the general claim that genera are always prior to species because they do not reciprocate as to the implication of being; cf. 15a4–6. For example, he says, if there is a fish (i.e. species) there is also an animal (i.e. genus); whereas if there is an animal it is not necessarily a fish. This example leaves the distinct impression that a genus (e.g. animal) might exist by itself independently of any particular species of that genus.[22] When formulated in this way, we can recognize it as a claim about the ontological priority of the genus, which Aristotle seems to reject in the *Metaphysics*. But here he appears to accept it unquestioningly as a legitimate result from applying the criterion of priority. Given the whole discussion in *Categories* 13, it would seem that he is committed to the view that the genus is prior by nature (τῇ φύσει) to the species.[23] This discussion is concerned with things that are simultaneous (ἅμα), as distinct from things that are prior and posterior, which is the topic of the previous chapter. Since they are complementary discussions, let us take a brief look at *Categories* 13.

Once again, I find the most interesting meaning of simultaneity to be that which is called "simultaneous by nature" (ἅμα τῇ φύσει). I think it is clear that this particular discussion of natural simultaneity both complements and clarifies the fifth meaning of natural priority in *Categories* 12, which was not included in the original count and, therefore, seems like an afterthought. My hunch is that the 'afterthought' is, in fact, the subsequent discussion of simultaneity by nature. Thus my interpretive strategy is to approach the meaning of natural priority indirectly by first examining Aristotle's account of the things that are called simultaneous by nature. What he says is that those things that reciprocate as to implication of being are called simultaneous by nature, provided that neither of them is the cause of being of the other.[24] There are a number of related points about this formulation that should be noted immediately. First, the language is almost identical with that used in the previous chapter for the corresponding criterion of priority, except for the absence of a negation word. Thus we might formulate the difference as follows: Those things that *do* reciprocate as to the implication of being are simultaneous by nature; whereas, among those things that do *not* thus reciprocate, one of them is prior to the other.

Even though Aristotle does not call this natural priority in *Categories* 12, such exact correspondence in language suggests that it is what he has in mind. Second, if we look at the examples given in each case, this suggestion tends to be reinforced. As an illustration of those things that are simultaneous by nature, Aristotle first mentions the double and the half. Since these are correlative concepts, as we might say, it is obvious how they reciprocate as to implication of being, in contrast to the one and the two (i.e. the examples given previously), which do not reciprocate in this manner.[25] Furthermore, he insists that neither the half nor the double is "the cause of being" (τὸ αἴτιον τοῦ εἶναι) of the other; cf. *Cat.*14b31–32. By contrast, the one may be assumed to be the cause of being for the number two, since one is the principle of numbers and principles are also causes. In this whole treatment of priority in the *Categories,* there is some evidence that the direction of formal causality, at least, may be determined by such criteria of priority.[26] On the basis of the same evidence, however, one might also claim that causal relationships are determining priority relations between things. This leads me to the third and most important point about the linguistic correspondence between the criteria for priority and simultaneity by nature. In the case of things that appear simultaneous by nature, the exception (i.e. if either is the cause of the other's being) turns out to be identical with the fifth kind of priority in *Categories* 12, which Aristotle says would "likely" be called priority by nature.[27]

Now this seems to conflict with my earlier claim that natural priority is usually found among those things that do *not* reciprocate as to implication of being. Here we have an instance of priority by nature being drawn from among those things that *do* reciprocate as to implication of being. Yet this does not directly contradict my claim because, as a general rule, such things are simultaneous by nature. In fact, only in exceptional circumstances when one of these things is the cause of the other do we have a case of natural priority.[28] Thus, as I have argued, the usual circumstances for natural priority are that things do not reciprocate as to implication of being. I think that my argument is supported by the way in which Aristotle presents the fifth kind of priority as if it were an exception to the general rule. Near the end of *Categories* 12 he has already completed his treatment of the four kinds of priority that were announced at the beginning, when he suddenly introduces what "seems to be" (δόξειε δ' ἂν . . . εἶναι) another way in which things are called prior. On account of the many senses of the verb δοκέω in Aristotle, it is difficult to ascertain whether or not he intends to express any hesitation in this report of linguistic phenomena. Perhaps some hesitation is found in the adverb εἰκότως later when he says that, among things that reciprocate as to implication of being, the thing that is in any way the cause of being (αἴτιον τοῦ εἶναι) of another could plausibly (εἰκότως) be called prior by nature.

Yet, he thinks it is clear (δῆλον) that there are such cases of priority and, in fact, he offers an example. The example, however, turns out to be something of a surprise insofar as it involves a relationship between things that appear to belong to different orders of being. Aristotle claims that "being a man" (τὸ εἶναι ἄνθρωπον) *does* reciprocate as to implication of being with a true statement about him (πρὸς τὸν ἀληθῆ περὶ αὐτοῦ λόγον); cf. *Cat.*14b14–15. By way of clarification, he explains that if there *is* a man (εἰ . . . ἔστιν ἄνθρωπος) then the statement in which we declare that there is a man turns out to be true. Furthermore, this is a reciprocal relationship because if the statement is true then there *is* a man. But from the point of view of causality this is *not* a reciprocal relation, since the true statement is in no way the cause of being of the thing (οὐδαμῶς αἴτιος τοῦ εἶναι τὸ πρᾶγμα). By contrast, the actual thing somehow seems (φαίνεταί πως) to be the cause of the statement being true. After all, as Aristotle explains, it is true on account of the being or the non-being of the thing (τῷ γὰρ εἶναι τὸ πρᾶγμα ἢ μὴ); cf. *Cat.* 14b18–22. Hence he concludes that this is a fifth way in which one thing is called prior to another.

In his commentary on this passage, Ackrill[29] finds it extremely odd that "the relation between facts and truth should be called a reciprocal implication of *existence*" (his italics). Of course, when formulated in this way, such a priority relation does appear rather odd but perhaps the appearance of oddity is produced by the formulation itself. For instance, in spite of the unqualified use of εἶναι in the Greek, I do not consider it appropriate to introduce the modern notion of 'existence' and so I prefer to talk about "the implication of being" (ἡ τοῦ εἶναι ἀκολούθησις). If we think in this way, it seems less strange to us when Aristotle says that "there being a man" (τὸ εἶναι ἄνθρωπον) reciprocates as to implication of being with the true statement about it; cf. *Cat.*14b14–15. We should also keep in mind that for Aristotle, as well as for Plato, truth and falsity are modes of being.[30] The lesson of the *Sophist* was that even not-being *is* in some sense. Obviously, it is impossible to substitute 'existence' for this 'is' and the same is true for any discussion of truth and falsity.

As Aristotle points out in *De Interpretatione,* falsity and truth have to do with combination and separation.[31] Furthermore, truth and falsity are essential differentiae of a statement-making sentence (ὁ ἀποφαντικὸς), as distinct from prayers or wishes; cf. *De Int.* 17a1–4. But every such sentence must contain either a verb or the inflexion of a verb; cf. 17a9–11. Even the definition of man, as Aristotle points out, is not yet a statement-making sentence (λόγος ἀποφαντικὸς) unless 'is' or 'will be' or 'was' or some such verb is added; cf. 17a11–12. Thus a *single* statement-making sentence is either one that reveals a single thing (ὁ ἓν δηλῶν) or is single in virtue of one connection (ὁ συνδέσμῳ εἷς); cf. *De Int.* 17a15–16. The latter, presumably, is what Aristotle calls a simple statement (ἡ ἁπλῆ ἀπόφανσις), which is one that affirms or denies something of something else (τὶ κατὰ τινος ἢ τὶ ἀπὸ τινος); cf. 17a20–21. Yet the statement that there is a man (ὅτι ἔστιν ἄνθρωπος) does not quite fit the model for simple predication, so it must be a statement-making sentence that reveals a single thing.

Now, we should be closer to understanding how the relationship between a fact and a true statement is reciprocal as to implication of being, while not being reciprocal with respect to causality. According to Aristotle's simple correspondence theory of truth, the fact that there is a man is revealed by the statement "there is a man." Conversely, if the statement is true, then it follows that there is a man but it does not follow that the true statement has somehow caused the state of affairs. Indeed, Aristotle insists that the true statement is not in any way (οὐδαμῶς) the cause of being for the thing. Yet, on the other hand, he concedes that the thing (τὸ πρᾶγμα) does in some way (πως) appear to be the cause of being true for the sentence (αἴτιον τοῦ εἶναι ἀληθῆ τὸν λόγον); cf. *Cat.*14b18–20. The Greek here shows that truth is being treated as a mode of being for which the thing is somehow responsible.[32] In order to make this more intelligible, I think that we should recall that for Aristotle truth in the primary sense exists in the soul; cf. *De Int.* 16a3–5. Thus truth depends primarily on the soul and is in some way caused by the soul. Given the nature of the Aristotelian soul, however, it cannot be the case that it produces truth without reference to things (πράγματα). A certain state of affairs must hold if the corresponding truth is to be intuited or demonstrated or, perhaps, known through induction by the soul. Hence, truth as a mode of being depends on that state of affairs and, thereby, is partly caused by it. Consequently, truth is in one way caused by the fact (or state of affairs) and in another way by the soul of the knower who grasps that fact and who thereby possesses the corresponding truth. Since a true statement merely symbolizes the condition of the soul, we can now see why Aristotle claims that the fact of there being a man is in some way the cause of the truth of the statement that there is a man.[33]

Still, in terms of his fourfold causality, I think that this sort of casuality must be classified as formal.[34] From my point of view, this is no accident, because such a kind of causality is most clearly inherited from Plato who tended to emphasize that the Forms as objects of knowledge are also the intelligible causes of sensible states of affairs. In addition, I think it is typical of the Platonic viewpoint to hold that the Forms are naturally prior both to the sensible things that participate in them and to the truths about them that are grasped by the human soul. With the Aristotelian emphasis upon immanent forms, I think that this viewpoint was modified into the position that sensible things (e.g. a man) are prior by nature to true statements about them (e.g. "there is a man"). But such a position still reflects the basic Platonic assumption that natural priority is dictated by the direction of formal causality. Perhaps Aristotle is conscious of this when he introduces the fifth meaning of priority in a rather tentative manner, as if he were reporting an inherited opinion.[35] Of course, such collecting of opinions is perfectly compatible with the stated purpose of listing the different meanings of priority, as he does in *Categories* 12.

Priority in Order and in Honor

To conclude this brief survey of the different meanings of priority outlined in the *Categories,* let me simply mention the two remaining senses that are not immediately relevant to my argument.[36] This neglect on my part is not intended to exclude the possibility that these senses may become important for understanding other aspects of Aristotle's thought. The third sense in which something is called prior is "according to some order" (κατά τινα τάξιν), such as is the case with sciences and speeches.[37] With reference to the first case, Aristotle says that in the demonstrative sciences there is a prior and posterior in order (τῇ τάξει). In geometry, for instance, the elements (τὰ στοιχεῖα) are prior in order to the propositions (τῶν διαγραμμάτων), just as the sound elements (τὰ στοιχεῖα) are prior to the syllables in grammar; cf. *Cat.*14a37–b2. The parallel with the priority of letters to syllables is noteworthy for a number of reasons. First, the linguistic evidence indicates that this is the source for the notion of 'element' (στοιχεῖον) that was adopted in the axiomatic sciences.[38] Second, the parallel itself suggests that Aristotle has in mind the priority by nature of something that is more intelligible absolutely, just as in the *Topics* passage already discussed; cf. *Top.*141b9–10.[39] This would fit the case of the demonstrative sciences, which first lay down principles and then proceed to prove propositions.

Similarly, in the case of speeches, the introduction (τὸ προοίμιον) is prior in order to the exposition (τῆς διηγέσεως); cf. *Cat.*14b2–3. The latter example of priority quite obviously depends on the conventions of rhetoric, yet we must not assume that it is purely arbitrary. Just as in the case of geometry, one might claim that there is a definite internal logic in a speech, quite as much as in a definition, that dictates that preliminary things should be stated first. Thus there are certain examples of this kind of priority with respect to some order (κατά τινα τάξιν) that might also be described in terms of logical priority, even though Aristotle does not do so. Even in *Metaphysics* Delta 11, as we shall see, he gives very little attention to this sense of priority with respect to some order.[40]

Finally, with reference to the *Categories,* let us turn to a fourth 'way' of priority that Aristotle seems rather reluctant to accept as a philosophical case of the priority relation. This is the sense according to which what is better (τὸ βέλτιον) and more honorable (τὸ τιμιώτερον) is thought to be prior by nature (πρότερον εἶναι τῇ φύσει δοκεῖ); cf. *Cat.*14b4–5. Judging from his offhand manner of treatment, Aristotle considers this sense of priority to be the least interesting philosophically. For example, he draws upon the language of the ordinary people (οἱ πολλοί) for the following example: people usually speak of those whom they honor more (τοὺς ἐντιμοτέρους) or love more (μᾶλλον ἀγαπωμένους) as 'being prior' (προτέρους); cf. *Cat.*14b5–7. In spite of the firm foundation this sense of priority has in ordinary Greek, Aristotle says that it is almost the most estranged (ἀλλοτριώτατος) of all the ways in which things are called prior. Now, for several reasons, it is difficult to know what to make of this remark.[41] For instance, it could mean that this is the least appropriate sense of priority or simply that it is further removed from the other senses. I prefer the latter interpretation because it would be most unusual for Aristotle to deny the appropriateness of a meaning that is embedded in ordinary language. Furthermore, it leaves open the possibility that this sense of priority may become important later when Aristotle considers the different ways in which the divine, as Prime Mover, may legitimately be called prior to everything else. But there is no evidence in the *Categories* that he has such a possibility in mind, unless we read a great deal into his use of the superlative of ἀλλότριος.[42] I think that, in general, his treatment of priority here does not contain those senses that turn out to be important for his own philosophical positions, rather it gives the meanings inherited from Plato almost exclusive attention.

Conclusion

In conclusion, I offer a tentative solution to the puzzle about why Aristotle ignores the distinction between primary and secondary substance in his treatment of different senses of priority.[43] By contrast with the usual ordering of the *Categories,* I suggest that chapters 12 and 13 were written *before* chapter 5 and that their conceptual background is characteristically Platonic.[44] I have already shown how the priority of genus to species, which is illustrated in chapter 13 with the animal/fish example, makes complete sense when seen against the background of Platonic division. But in chapter 5 this order of priority is implicitly denied in the following way:

> But as the primary substances stand to the other things, so the species stands to the genus: the species is a subject for the genus (for the genera are predicated of the species but the species are not predicated reciprocally of the genera). Hence for this reason too the species is more a substance than the genus.[45]

The contrast with chapter 13 is much clearer in the Greek when Aristotle explains that the genera are predicated of the species, whereas the species are not predicated reciprocally of the genera.[46] The use of the word ἀντιστρέφει provides us with a vital clue to the revision of the order of priority between genus and species that is going on here. With the introduction of the Aristotelian notion of predication, this order is entirely reversed over against that associated with Platonic division. The new paradigm is the primacy of the individual thing that can serve as a subject of predication for both essential and accidental predicates. But in the above passage, this model of predication is also extended to the relationship between species and genus, so that the first is held to be prior in substance to the second. Even though he explicitly prohibits us from thinking of different degrees of substance at the same level, he still accepts a relationship of priority among substances in general when he says that the species is more a substance than the genus (τὸ εἶδος τοῦ γένους μᾶλλον οὐσία).[47] My conjecture is that this latter concession reflects the Platonic identification of what is more substantial with what is more intelligible, whereas the former prohibition represents Aristotle's own attempt to break with the view that the most universal things are the most substantial. This is one reason why the *Categories* remains such a fascinating yet inconsistent work.

3

The Senses of Priority in *Metaphysics* Delta

WHEN WE LOOK UNDER 'PRIORITY' IN THE PHILOSOPHICAL DICTIONARY[1] THAT constitutes *Metaphysics* Delta, we find a more comprehensive treatment of priority and posteriority. It is not merely the addition of the correlative concept 'posterior' that represents an advance over the *Categories* but, even more so, the clear attempt on the part of Aristotle to systematize the meanings of 'prior' under a number of different headings. This is what I take him to be doing when he begins with the assumption that "in each genus" (ἐν ἑκάστῳ γένει) there is something that is a first or a principle (ὡς ὄντος τινὸς πρώτου καὶ ἀρχῆς); cf. *Met.*1018b9–10. From what follows, I think it is clear that the genera he has in mind are identical with some of the categories. Assuming there is a principle in each genus, Aristotle says, a thing may be called "prior" because it is nearer to some principle (ἐγγύτερον ἀρχῆς τινὸς) that is determined in one of the following ways: (i) absolutely (ἁπλῶς) or by nature (τῇ φύσει); (ii) with reference to something (πρός τι); (iii) or somewhere (που); (iv) or by some people (ὑπὸ τινων). It cannot be completely accidental that some of these ways happen to coincide with Aristotle's categories of relation (πρός τι) and place (που). Subsequently, we find time (ποτέ) being added to these ways in which a principle is determined, and it is possible that the first (i) way hints at the category of substance.[2] While it stands for some natural or absolute determination, the other three (ii–iv) represent different ways in which a principle may be determined in a relative fashion. Within such a categorical framework,[3] Aristotle proceeds to elucidate a number of different senses of "the prior and the posterior" (τὸ πρότερον καὶ τὸ ὕστερον). Once again, I will begin with my translation of the relevant texts before proceeding with the exegesis.

Translation of *Metaphysics* Delta 11

Some things are called prior and posterior, on the one hand, (I) when there is something first and a principle in each genus, by virtue of being[4] closer to some principle that is determined either absolutely and by nature or relative to something or to somewhere or by some people. For example, (*a*) with respect to place (things are called prior) by virtue of being closer to some place either determined by nature, e.g. the middle or the extremity, or with reference to some chance thing; whereas what is further away is posterior. (*b*) With respect to time (things are also called prior) by virtue of being further from the present moment in the case of past events; just as, for example, the Trojan war is prior to the Persian Wars because it is further (in time) from the present. In the case of future events, however, (things are called prior) by virtue of being closer to the present moment; just as, for example, the Nemean are prior to the Pythian Games because they are closer [to the present moment].[5] (In both cases) we used[6] the present moment as a principle and as something first. (*c*) With respect to motion (things are called prior) because that which is closer to the first mover is prior; e.g. the child (is prior) to the man. For this[7] too is a kind of principle taken absolutely. (*d*) With respect to power (things are called prior) because that which exceeds by virtue of power and what is more powerful is prior. Such is that (person) whose decision it is necessary for the other, i.e. the inferior,[8] to follow. Thus, if the first does not move neither is the latter moved but when he moves the other is moved. The decision is a principle. (*e*) With respect to order (things are called prior) that have been arranged according to a certain ratio with reference to one determinate thing. For instance, the second man (in the chorus) is prior to the third or the penultimate string (on a lyre) to the last string. In the former case, the chorus leader is a principle, while it is the middle string in the latter case.

These things, therefore, are called prior in this way but in another way (II) that which is prior in knowledge is (said to be) prior without qualification. Among these there is a distinction between those things (which are called prior) (*a*) with respect to account[9] and (*b*) with respect to sensation. With respect to account, also, the accident is prior to the whole; for example, the musical is prior to the musical man, since there will not be a whole account without its part. But yet there cannot be a musical without it being a musical something. Furthermore, those things are called prior which are the attributes of prior things. For instance, straightness is prior to planeness because the first is a *per se* attribute of a line, whereas the second (belongs in this way) to a plane.[10]

While these things are called prior and posterior in this way, other things (are called prior and posterior) (III) with respect to nature and substance when they can be without others, whereas the others cannot be without them—Plato used this as a division. But, since being has many senses, first (*a*) the subject is prior and therefore substance is prior. Second, (*b*) in another sense, (things are called prior) with respect to potency and with respect to actuality. While some things are prior with respect to potency, other things are prior with respect to actuality. For example, with respect to potency, the half line is prior to the whole line and the part is prior to the whole and the matter is prior to the substance; whereas they are posterior with respect to actuality, since each will be in actuality only after the dissolution of the other.

Hence, in some way, all the things called prior and posterior are spoken of with respect to these. For, with respect to generation, it is possible for some things to be without others, e.g. the whole without the parts; while, with respect to destruction (it is also possible), e.g. the part without the whole. And similarly for all the others.

Priority as Dictated by a Principle

There are five senses of priority grouped together initially by Aristotle because they share the common feature of being judged in relation to some principle under whatever genus they fall.[11] First (*a*) with respect to place (κατὰ τόπον), a thing may be called prior because it is nearer to some place that is determined either (i) by nature (τῇ φύσει) or (ii) with reference to some chance thing (πρὸς τὸ τυχόν). In illustrating what he means by a place that is naturally determined, Aristotle makes a rather ambiguous reference to "the center or the extremity" (τοῦ μέσου ἢ τοῦ ἐσχάτου). Of course this could refer to any circle but, if he intends to satisfy the conditions for a place that is naturally determined by its very being, he must be referring to the center and outermost boundary of the physical universe as he conceives of it.[12] Thus, within the category of place, Aristotle thinks there are places that are absolutely determined by nature and with reference to which we can say that some things are prior to others. In an Aristotelian universe, for example, one can say that αἰθήρ is prior to ἀήρ with reference to the external boundary and that it is also posterior to it, if we take the center of the universe as our absolute reference point. We could be misled by the apparent relativity involved here, if we equate it with taking *any* chance place or thing as our point of reference. But whatever is closer (ἐγγύτερον) to the center of the universe is prior by nature, whereas the thing that is closest to our dwelling house is only prior by accident. Similarly, with respect to a place determined by nature, the thing that is farthest away from the center is posterior (τὸ δὲ πορρώτερον ὕστερον) in a sense that is different from what is farthest removed from us or any chance place, which is posterior in an accidental manner. Of course, given his rejection of the Atomistic world view, Aristotle does not accept the possibility that what is closest to the earth is accidentally, rather than naturally, prior. In addition, he does want to claim that the first moved thing at the internal boundary of the universe is prior in some natural sense. Perhaps this is his reason for holding on to two natural and absolute points of reference for priority with respect to place.[13]

Since Aristotle's outline of the different senses of priority in *Metaphysics* Delta is very short on detail, I think we must look elsewhere for examples and clarification of each of these kinds of priority. For instance, in his treatise on time in *Physics* Delta, Aristotle makes an assertion about priority in place that may help to explain why it is listed here before priority in time. The context for this assertion is provided by a discussion of why we perceive motion and time together. According to Aristotle, our perception of time depends on our perception of some motion, either external or internal to the mind; cf. *Phy.* 219a3ff. He argues that the fact of motion being from something to something else makes it dependent on magnitude. Since the latter is continuous, motion also will be continuous and, as a result, so will time. This series of dependencies is taken to establish another series that goes as follows:

> Now the prior or the posterior are attributes primarily of a place, and in virtue of position. So since the prior and the posterior exist in magnitudes, they must also exist in motions and be analogous to those in magnitudes; and further, the prior and the posterior exist also in time because time always follows a motion.[14]

There are a number of noteworthy things about this passage, especially if we view it in conjunction with *Metaphysics* Delta 11, where priority with respect to place is given a prominent initial position. If we did not make such a cross-check with the *Physics* we might not attach any significance to the order in which the different senses of priority are listed. In view of our previous discussion of the *Categories,* however, what is surprising is the complete reversal of statements in that work about priority in time being the principal meaning of priority. Incidentally, this reversal is not explicitly acknowledged in Delta 11, and to find it there at all we must read it into the ordering of senses. Be that as it may, what is further clarified by the *Physics* passage is that the principle of ordering for priority with respect to place is position (θέσις), whether this be relative or absolute. Thus, as he says in Delta 11, things may be prior with respect to place by virtue of being nearer (τῷ εἶναι ἐγγύτερον) to some place determined either naturally or by chance. This determinate position is what serves as a principle (ἀρχή) in terms of which things are judged either prior or posterior with reference to place, depending on whether they are nearer to it or further away from it.[15]

It would seem, however, that there are no absolute reference points for the second sense of priority (*b*) with respect to time (κατὰ χρόνον). We recall that this was given pride of place in the *Categories* where it was said to be the strictest (κυριώτατον) meaning of priority. There also Aristotle seems to have taken the present moment as a privileged point of reference with respect to which one thing may be called older (and hence prior) to another because it is a greater distance in time from the present. This privileged reference point is retained in *Metaphysics* Delta but some further subtleties are added to the account of priority with respect to future time. With regard to past events, Aristotle explains, we call "prior" those that are furthest from the present (πορρώτερον τοῦ νῦν); e.g. the Trojan War is prior in this sense to the Persian Wars. By contrast, with respect to future events, we call "prior" whatever is closer to the present (ἐγγύτερον τοῦ νῦν); e.g. the Nemean Games are prior in this sense to the Pythian Games because they are nearer to the present time. Aristotle seems to think that the reason for the apparent conflict in results is that we used "the now" as a principle and as something first.[16] This statement leaves the impression that "the now" is being treated as a fixed and absolute point of reference like the center or boundary of the universe. Yet the very nature of the present moment in time precludes this because it is constantly changing and, if we assume time to be linear, moving forward in a single direction.[17] Thus, at one point in time, the Nemean Games are prior to the Pythean Games but at a different "now" they may be posterior to them. Contrary to the initial impression given by Aristotle, it is not the case that "the now" gives us an absolute and natural point of reference for determining what is prior and posterior with respect to time, for it is more like a chance point of reference that is relative to us.[18] But it should be noted that, in the present treatment, he makes no effort to clarify how the principle for priority in time is determined.[19]

If we turn again to the treatise on time in the *Physics,* however, we can find some further elaboration on these points with regard to priority in time. We have already noted how Aristotle has changed his mind in making it a sense of priority that is derivative from priority in place through priority in motion. Basically, his argument is that we recognize time when we limit motion by means of a prior and a posterior.[20] In other words, we say that time has elapsed (γεγονέναι χρόνον) when we grasp through perception a prior and posterior in motion. Now, I think it would be mistaken and anachronistic to conclude from these passages that Aristotle considered time to be completely dependent upon our perception, even though he gives many tantalizing hints in that direction. It would be more correct to say that he makes time dependent upon motion and then draws upon our experience of time to support that position.

For confirmation of the inseparable link between motion and time, let us look at another passage in *Physics* Delta 14 that elucidates the strange reversal of priorities that takes place when 'the now' is used as a principle of ordering with reference both to past and future time:

> But what exists prior to another exists in time, for things are said to be prior or posterior in virtue of their time interval from the present moment, which is the boundary of the past and the future; so since the moments are in time, also the prior and the posterior will be in time, for that in which the moments exist is also that in which the time intervals between the moments exist. But the term "prior" with reference to the past is used in a manner contrary to that with reference to the future; for, with reference to the past, we call "prior" that which is further from the present moment, and we call "posterior" that which is nearer; while with reference to the future, we call "prior" that which is nearer to the present moment, and we call "posterior" that which is further.[21]

This passage is given its context by Aristotle's defense of his claim that every change or everything in motion is also in time. Very briefly, his argument is that the faster or slower exists with respect to every change and the very concept of 'faster in motion' entails that something changes into a subject before something else. The above passage picks up the argument at this point and asserts that whatever exists prior to another is in time.[22] Subsequent to the quoted passage, the argument concludes that every change and every motion is in time because the prior is in time and every motion must have a prior in it. Now, contrary to his previous claims in *Physics* Delta 11, this argument gives the strong impression that he is making priority in motion dependent upon priority in time. This may help us to clear up a puzzle in his subsequent outline of priority with respect to motion, but for the moment, I have no way of resolving this apparent inconsistency.[23] What I do want to note about the above-quoted passage is the way in which Aristotle takes great pains to spell out that 'the now,' as a principle of priority in time, yields opposite results depending on whether one is considering past or future time.

So far in *Metaphysics* Delta, when he talks about what is prior and posterior with respect to place and time, Aristotle seems to be sticking to his own categorical framework. But it is difficult to see what "genus" is involved in the subsequent sense of priority (*c*) with respect to motion (κατὰ κίνησιν). Since change can come under a number of different categories, we need some more definite indication of whether Aristotle means change in substance or quality or quantity or place.[24] He does not help us very much with his explanation to the effect that those things are prior that are nearer the first mover,[25] nor is the matter clarified by the example he offers; i.e. that the child is prior to the man. Perhaps a hint can be found in Aristotle's subsequent statement that this is a sort of principle, taken absolutely (ἀρχὴ δέ καὶ αὕτη τις ἁπλῶς). The use of the word ἁπλῶς here seems to suggest that he is referring to substantial change, but if that were the case, his example would surely say that the man is prior to the child. The fact that he says the opposite indicates that he has something else in mind. In order to make some sense of this puzzling passage, it is crucial to identify the principle (ἀρχή) with reference to which things are being called prior and posterior, since this is an essential part of the framework established at the beginning of Delta 11.

It is in terms of this framework that we should understand his talk about something being "nearer to the primary bringer of change" (ἐγγύτερον τοῦ πρώτου κινήσαντος) as a *general* formula for priority with respect to all kinds of change.[26] Therefore, in each particular genus, we must identify the first mover as a principle for determining priority relations within that category. For instance, in the case of living substances, Aristotle identifies the adult male as the primary bringer of substantial change *qua* impregnator of the female. It is very tempting to think that this must be what he is referring to with his example of the man and the boy, but the grammar of the passage resists such a construal.[27] Another possibility, which is suggested by Apostle, is that the example should be understood under the category of action or of "doing" (ποιεῖν). If that were the case, however, we would have to imagine a situation in which a man gives a message or an order to a boy (or a slave) who transmits it to somebody else or moves something else. In that special case the boy would be prior (to the other people or things moved) because of being nearer to the man, who is the principle of action. While this provides us with a legitimate Aristotelian example of priority with respect to change, it does not seem to fit the text as we have it. Perhaps the problem of interpretation arises from Aristotle's attempt to squeeze a very general formula into a brief passage, together with a single representative example.[28]

Similar difficulties for my assumption of a categorical framework arise from the subsequent sense of priority with respect to capacity (κατὰ δύναμιν). If δύναμις is taken in the broader sense as "potentiality," then it is applicable to many categories; yet if it is taken in the narrower sense as "power," it is not obvious that it falls under any particular category.[29] In this case, however, the example of priority that is given seems to require the narrower sense because it illustrates the priority of whatever exceeds in power (τὸ ὑπερέχον τῇ δυνάμει) or of what is more powerful (τὸ δυνατώτερον). For instance, that person is prior in power whose decision determines the actions of another who is therefore posterior (ὕστερον) in the same sense; cf. *Met.* 1018b22–24. The example seems to presuppose the social ranking of the people involved or perhaps it refers to the role of a leader vis-à-vis his followers. Aristotle sums up this type of priority in the following condensed fashion: where the one (i.e. the prior) is not moving, then the other (i.e. the posterior) is not moved, but when the first moves then the second also is moved.[30] Here the decision is the principle (ἡ δὲ προαίρεσις ἀρχή), as Aristotle explains, while possibly playing upon the ambiguity of the word ἀρχή.[31]

In order to clarify what he has in mind, it might be useful to look at one of the senses of 'principle' he lists in *Metaphysics* Delta 1. This is the sense in which there is a starting point with respect to decision (κατὰ προα ίρεσιν) that changes things that are changed (κινεῖται τὰ κινούμεθα) and alters things that are suddenly altered (μεταβάλλει τὰ μεταβάλλοντα); cf. *Met.* 1013a10–11. By way of illustration, Aristotle suggests that this is the reason why the leaders for cities (αἵ κατα πόλεις ἀρχαὶ) and the potentates (αἱ δυναστεῖαι) and the kings and tyrants are all called ἀρχαί. Similarly, the arts (αἱ τέχναι) and especially the architectonic arts are called ἀρχαί, presumably because the decision of the artist is a principle of change or of motion in other things. Thus, I think it is quite clear that this sense of ἀρχή with respect to decision has a direct bearing on the sense of priority I am trying to explicate.

Since this is called priority with respect to power (κατὰ δύναμιν), it will also prove useful to look at the different senses of 'power' listed in Delta 12. What we find is that the very first meaning of power fits our needs because it is equivalent to a principle of change or of motion (ἀρχή κινήσεως ἢ μεταβολῆς) that is either in something other than the thing moved or in the thing itself but qua other; cf. *Met.* 1019a15ff.[32] For instance, the art of building is a power that belongs to the builder rather than in the thing that is built. Yet the art of healing might belong as a power in the man who is being healed (e.g. if the physician is healing himself) but not qua patient. In both cases the decision to build or to heal is prior to the building or the healing, so that these can serve as examples of priority according to power and with reference to decision. Incidentally, these also can be used to illustrate priority with respect to change.[33] What this overlapping tends to suggest is that Aristotle is drawing upon other headings in his philosophical dictionary (which covers many of the categories) for different meanings of priority that are determined with reference to a principle.

Until we examine the illustrations provided for the final meaning of priority listed under this heading, we might assume that it is taken directly from the *Categories*.[34] This is called priority with respect to order (κατὰ τάξιν), yet it seems that the principle itself is not determined absolutely (ἁπλῶς) but with reference to something (πρός τι). I think that this becomes clear when Aristotle explains that priority with respect to order is present whenever things are arranged at intervals according to a certain ratio and with reference to some definite thing.[35] Here I have doubts about the usual translations of λόγος as "formula" (Apostle and Kirwan) or as "rule" (Ross) because I am convinced that the language refers to intervals set according to a certain ratio (λόγος).[36] This is confirmed further by the musical examples he uses to illustrate priority with respect to order or arrangement. In the Greek chorus the second man (παραστάτης) is ranked as being prior to the third man (τριτοστάτου), while the next-to-lowest string (παρανήτη) on the lyre is taken to be prior to the lowest (νήτη); cf. *Met.*1018b26–29. In the first case, the leader of the chorus (ὁ κορυφαῖος) is the principle (ἀρχή) with reference to which the order of priority is decided; whereas such an order is determined with reference to the middle string (μέση) of the lyre in the second case. In each case the principle is not itself determined in an absolute fashion but rather relative to something.

If one were to choose from among the three options for relative determination set out at the beginning of Delta 11, I think that the most appropriate might be the last one; i.e. (iv) determination by some people (ὑπό τινων). It could be argued that the ranking of the chorus in Greek drama was a result of the conventions established by the people involved in this activity. Similarly it is plausible to claim that the ordering of the strings on the lyre was a convention established among musicians.[37] It is not clear, however, what Aristotle has in mind when he says that the principle is determined relative to a single thing (πρός τι ἓν ὡρισμένον). Perhaps he is not here concerned with how the principle itself is determined but only with how things are established as prior or posterior relative to a single determinate principle. If we compare this with his treatment of priority according to some order (κατὰ τινα τάξιν) in the *Categories,* we find a similar lack of specificity as to whether the ordering principle itself is naturally or conventionally determined. On this question, however, it is enlightening to compare the examples given in each treatment. Just as in the example of the Greek chorus, an argument could be made for the conventional nature of the principle that determines the order of priority in speeches such that the introduction always comes before the exposition. Even in the case of the sciences, a similar argument could be made that the priority of the so-called elements (i.e. axioms and definitions) is established conventionally by mathematicians. Yet, as I have already pointed out, Aristotle would probably think that there is a strong logical basis for such priority, even if the ordering principle were itself established by some people (ὑπό τινων), such as mathematicians and rhetoricians. But, once again, this is speculation on my part in the absence of a clear statement.

Priority with Respect to Knowledge

Having listed the senses of priority defined with reference to a principle, Aristotle makes a very clear transition to a cluster of priorities that are defined with reference to knowledge; cf. *Met.*1018b29–31. Under this heading of priority in acquaintance (τὸ τῇ γνώσει πρότερον), things are called prior in an absolute sense (ἁπλῶς). Among things that are said to be prior for knowledge in this general sense, he distinguishes further between priority with respect to account (κατὰ τὸν λόγον) and priority with respect to perception (κατὰ τὴν αἴσθησιν); cf. 1018b31–32.[38] Aristotle seems to think that in most cases these two approaches yield conflicting results because, by way of elucidation, he says that the universals (τὰ καθόλου) are prior with respect to account, whereas the particulars (τὰ καθ' ἕκαστα) are prior with respect to perception; cf. 1018b32–34. On the face of it, this would appear to be another version of his famous distinction between what is prior and more knowable to us (πρὸς ἡμᾶς) and what is prior and better known by nature (τῇ φύσει).[39] Given our previous analysis of this distinction in the *Topics* and the *Posterior Analytics,* we might feel justified in assuming that in *Metaphysics* Delta universals are still held to be prior in an unqualified sense with respect to knowledge, while particulars are prior in the same sense with respect to perception.

But contrary to our expectations, the distinction is not developed here in such terms. Instead, what we find is that priority with respect to account is elucidated in terms of accidents and wholes as follows: the accident (τὸ συμβεβηκὸς) is prior to the whole (τοῦ ὅλου); for example, the musical (τὸ μουσικὸν) is prior to 'the musical man' (τοῦ μουσικοῦ ἀνθρώπου); cf. *Met.*1018b34–35. Aristotle's justification for this sense of priority is rendered in terms of simple addition; i.e. it would not be possible to have the whole account (ὁ λόγος ὅλος) without its parts. Of course not, one might object, but the genus 'animal' is not a part of 'man' in the same sense that 'musical' is part of 'musical man.'[40] Aristotle would probably agree, but for reasons best known to himself, he concentrates on the accidental relationship of an attribute to a subject when giving an example of priority with respect to account. Perhaps this is a special sense of priority which, as we shall see in chapter five, turns out to be useful for his response to mathematical Platonism in Mu 2. But, in addition to this, I think there are clear indications of a shift in his thinking about the priority of the universal over the particular. For instance, while conceding that 'musical' is prior to 'musical man' with respect to account, he warns that musicality cannot exist unless there is someone who is musical.[41] In other words, musicality is an attribute that cannot exist apart from some subject that presumably is self-subsistent. The implications of this caveat are not spelled out in *Metaphysics* Delta, but we shall find that they become important later.[42] It should be noted, however, that the question of priority is much more complex in the case of essential attributes like rationality, for instance, and their relation to a subject like man.

The next sense of priority which Aristotle lists is rather puzzling in a number of ways. For example, it does not appear to have any clear connection with the senses of priority that are listed before and after it. Thus, some modern commentators[43] assume that it is a separate sense of priority which is outlined in the following passage:

(3) Again, the attributes of prior things are called "prior"; for example, straightness is prior to planeness. For the first is an essential *attribute* of a line, the second of a surface.[44]

Since the passage begins with the word ἔτι, Apostle naturally takes it to be introducing a new and separate sense of priority, and on first glance, this appears to be correct. The previous sense was described with reference to knowledge and was divided into priority with respect to account and priority with respect to perception. We can certainly exclude the possibility that straightness (εὐθύτης) might be called prior to planeness (λειότητος) with respect to perception, since the plane is more obvious to the senses, as Aristotle says in *Topics* 141b6ff. From our analysis of that passage, however, we should recall that there is another sense in which the line is prior to the plane because it is more intelligible absolutely (ἁπλῶς γνωριμώτερον). I think that this sense of priority is presupposed here because already one must have some criterion for the priority of 'things' like lines and planes before one can order their attributes in terms of priority, as Aristotle tries to do here.

Thus I would argue that this should be seen as a kind of priority with reference to knowledge, which therefore belongs with the previous cluster of priorities.[45] Since it does not fit under priority with respect to perception, it should come under priority with respect to formula (κατὰ τὸν λόγον) when this is interpreted broadly enough. The wider meaning of λόγος that seems appropriate here is "account," because one can plausibly assert that some account must be given of the line before the plane becomes fully intelligible. This kind of priority with respect to account is illustrated by Euclid's *Elements,* where the definition of a line is prior to that of a plane and where plane geometry is prior to solid geometry. I think that it is within the context of an assumed priority among these demonstrative sciences that we must understand Aristotle's very brief explanation to the effect that straightness is prior to planeness because it is a *per se* attribute (καθ᾽ αὐτὴν πάθος) of a line, whereas the latter belongs primarily to a plane. As we know from the *Posterior Analytics,* scientific knowledge requires that one identify the primary subject to which attributes like straightness belong *per se.*[46] Hence, while it may be obvious to the senses that a surface is straight-edged, this fact can only be scientifically explained in terms of the characteristic straightness of a line. In general, therefore, the priority of straightness to planeness might be described as logical, and this fits nicely with Aristotle's response to the mathematical ontology of the Platonists, which I will consider in my final chapter.

Priority in Nature or Substance

At this point in the outline of different meanings, Aristotle's text once again contains a clear transition to another sense of priority:

> Objects, then, are called "prior" and "posterior" in the manner stated, but (4) others are called so with respect to nature or *substance,* when some things can exist without the others, but not conversely—a distinction used by Plato.[47]

Apostle's translation indicates by its numbering that this is the fourth distinct meaning of priority, but if we count the transitions in the Greek text, it is actually the third distinct group of meanings.[48] More noteworthy than the numbering of senses, however, is the fact that this is the only place in the whole treatment where a particular meaning of priority is associated with a historical figure. I find it particularly significant that the criterion of priority explicitly attributed to Plato here is quite similar to the one we have already encountered in the account of priority given at *Categories* 12 and 13.[49] Thus it should come as no surprise to us that what satisfies this criterion is called prior "with respect to nature" (κατὰ φύσιν). But it is perhaps a little surprising to find Aristotle apparently accepting a Platonic criterion for what is prior with respect to substance ((κατὰ) οὐσίαν), especially in one of the books of the *Metaphysics*. In order to resolve this puzzle, let us begin by examining the language of the criterion itself, which, ideally, should be doctrinally neutral if it is to serve its purpose as a judging device.

The criterion dictates that those things are prior with respect to nature and substance "which can be without other things, while others cannot be without them."[50] The whole criterion has a formulaic ring to it, just like the criterion of nonreciprocity as to implication of being that we examined in the *Categories*. In fact, I think it can be argued that the two criteria yield identical results insofar as they use the test of nonreciprocity on two *related* things in order to determine which of them is prior by nature.[51] Even though no illustrations of any sort are given along with the criterion in the *Metaphysics* passage, it is still clear that its application could yield the natural priority of the unit to the point and of the point to the line, etc. But it is important to note that, in order to get this result, one must supply the assumption that the order of being follows the order of knowledge. This may help us to understand why Aristotle takes the unusual step of saying that this division (διαίρεσις) was used by Plato. Ross[52] has noted that there seems to be no passage in Plato where this "distinction" is drawn, and therefore, he conjectures that Aristotle is thinking of some oral utterance of his master.[53] However, I think it is unnecessary to appeal to the so-called unwritten doctrines here because there is a way in which this criterion of priority can be seen as essential to the method of division (διαίρεσις) that is used in dialogues like the *Sophist* and *Statesman*.

In order to show this, let me recall the passage in *Categories* 13 where Aristotle seems to claim that genera are always prior to species because they do not reciprocate as to implication of being; cf. 15a4–6. Within that context it is clear that natural priority is meant, since those things that *do* reciprocate as to implication of being are called simultaneous by nature (ἅμα τῇ φύσει). Furthermore, a leading example of such simultaneity is provided by the coordinate species of the same genus. In fact, as Aristotle explains, such species as bird and beast and fish are coordinate precisely because they are the results of the same division (κατὰ τὴν αὐτὴν διαίρεσιν); cf. 14b34–36. By contrast, the genus of animal is prior to all of these species because it does not reciprocate with them as to implication of being. It is not hard to see that this would be a very important consideration for the philosophical dialectician, as portrayed in the *Sophist* and *Statesman,* who wishes to carve up reality at its natural joints; i.e. according to its genera and species. It would be a poor butcher indeed who did not realize that there is a single generic whole that has to be first brought into view before it can be carved up into a limited number of natural divisions.[54] For Plato, the fact that definitions can be found through division simply follows from the natural priorities among things. Thus I think one can make a rather convincing case for the claim that, in *Metaphysics* Delta 11, Aristotle is referring to the Platonic method of division.[55]

We can gain further insight into the characteristic application of the Platonic criterion given here by adducing some parallel passages where such a criterion is clearly being used. For instance, within a dialectical context at *Metaphysics* Beta 5, the body (τὸ σῶμα) is said to be less substantial (ἧττον οὐσία) than the surface (τῆς ἐπιφανείας), and the plane less so than the line.[56] The reason given is that these defining boundaries of the body are thought to be capable of 'existing' without body, whereas the body cannot be without them.[57] I think it is fairly clear from the language used here that this is a concrete application of the criterion of priority with respect to nature and substance, which is credited to Plato in Delta 11. A similar application can be found in Delta 8, where the different meanings of substance (οὐσία) are outlined. One of these senses is said to hold for those constituent parts that define and signify a 'this,' since their destruction would lead to the destruction of the whole.[58] For example, Aristotle reports, some people claim that the plane has this relationship to body and that the line has a similar relationship to the plane. The logical conclusion for this way of thinking is to make number prior in substance to everything else because, if it were eliminated, there would be nothing without its contribution of defining everything.[59] Aristotle reports that such a general conclusion is drawn by some people but he does not positively identify them. For my purposes, however, it is sufficient to note that the conclusion is consistent with an application of the criterion of priority with respect to nature and substance, which is attributed explicitly to Plato.[60]

Thus far in his account of priority in Delta 11, I think it is fair to say that Aristotle has merely listed the various meanings that were available in the Greek language itself and in the philosophical tradition that he consciously inherits. But, to return to a puzzle that I have raised previously, it is difficult to see how he can accept without demur the Platonic meaning of priority with respect to nature and substance, which we have just discussed. As we might expect, however, there is a definite attempt to establish his own perspective in the subsequent passage:

Since "to be" has many senses, first the underlying subject is prior, and hence a substance is prior. Second, in another sense objects are called "prior" and "posterior" with respect to potentiality and actuality; for some objects are prior with respect to potentiality, others with respect to actuality. For example, with respect to potentiality, the half line is said to be prior to the whole line, the part prior to the whole, and matter prior to substance, but with respect to actuality they are posterior; for they will actually exist after decomposition.[61]

In both their editions of the *Metaphysics*, Jaeger and Ross treat this whole passage as if it were parenthetical to the previous passage that outlined the criterion of priority with respect to nature and substance. Now, while there is a way in which this is correct, it may also prove to be misleading. For instance, it does not take sufficient account of the shift in perspective that is introduced with the words τὸ εἶναι πολλαχῶς. This has much the same meaning as the characteristic phrase τὸ ὂν λέγεται πολλαχῶς that is frequently used by Aristotle in contexts where he is presenting his own views on substance; cf. *Metaphysics* E2 and Z1. While keeping this in mind, however, we should also retain the link with the previous passage because he obviously wants to apply the criterion for priority in substance within his own perspective.[62] I think that this is what he is driving at in his claim that the subject is prior and therefore substance is prior.[63] Ross[64] takes this to be simply an application of the distinction between substance and the other categories, since these represent different senses of being. But I do not see how this can be correct because Aristotle clearly *argues* for the priority of substance when he uses the word διὸ. Thus it must be the case that he is applying the previous criterion to yield the priority of the substratum and arguing from this result *to* the priority of substance.[65] Let us see how this works.

There is a very real sense in which this brief argument encapsulates the whole argument of *Metaphysics* Zeta, yet I must postpone consideration of this book to my final chapter. Here I will simply pick up some threads of the argument from Zeta 3, where I see a strong similarity with the present argument. The chapter begins with a parallel assertion that 'substance' has, if not many senses, at least four special meanings.[66] Since we know from Zeta 1 that Aristotle focuses the general question about what is being upon the specific question about what is substance, we have here a close parallel with the statement that 'being' is said in many senses. The fact that both passages are concerned with substance makes the parallel more exact. Among its four candidates for substance, Zeta 3 lists "the underlying subject" (τὸ ὑποκείμενον) that at Delta 11 is judged to be prior with respect to nature and substance, according to the Platonic criterion of priority. We can better understand this rather surprising result by looking at the extra information about τὸ ὑποκείμενον that is supplied in Zeta 3. For instance, the underlying subject is described as "that of which other things are predicated, while it itself is not predicated of anything else."[67] This clearly establishes a relationship of ontological dependency between the subject and its predicated attributes. Hence, by applying the criterion from Delta 11, one might claim that the underlying subject is prior in substance because it can 'exist' without them, whereas they cannot 'exist' without it.[68] In fact, Aristotle says something similar about primary substances in *Categories* 5 when he concludes that if they did not 'exist' it would be impossible for other things to 'exist.'[69] Furthermore, this is said by way of conclusion to a discussion about the role of primary substance as the subject of all predicates; cf. *Cat.* 2a34 ff.

Thus, in *Metaphysics* Zeta 3, it is quite natural for Aristotle to begin his inquiry into substance with the underlying subject because, as he explains, "the primary subject is thought to be substance especially."[70] Yet things do not turn out to be as simple as they appear initially because 'subject' has at least three senses; i.e. matter, form, and the composite of both. The rest of Book Zeta is taken up with the task of determining which of these is the primary sense of substance, while also considering the other candidates for substance such as the universal and the genus. Without going into the conclusions of that book in detail, I think it is true to say that Aristotle never changes his mind about substance being the primary subject of attributes. Thus, in the argument at Delta 11, it is typical for him to conclude that substance is prior from the assumed fact that the primary subject is prior. Indeed, the assumption itself is almost tautological (for how can a *primary* subject fail to be prior in some important sense) and the conclusion must have seemed intuitive to Aristotle. Yet, a definite shift in the notion of 'priority' (as compared with the Platonic meaning) has taken place with the introduction of an underlying subject of predication. For one thing, the Platonic system of dependencies will be radically changed because everything is now made to depend upon a primary substance, such as an individual man, which is the ultimate subject of all predicates.[71] Thus, while applying an ostensibly Platonic criterion, Aristotle can arrive at completely different conclusions about priority with respect to nature and substance. This is fairly typical of his general dialectical strategy.

Priority with Respect to Potentiality and Actuality

I would suggest also that an analogous shift occurs with the introduction of the notions of potentiality and actuality. I think it is quite generally accepted that in their technical senses these are characteristically Aristotelian concepts that do not appear in Plato.[72] So, at Delta 11, when Aristotle begins to talk about priority with respect to potentiality and actuality (κατὰ δύναμιν καὶ κατ' ἐντελέχειαν), it is fairly safe to assume that he wants to introduce a new perspective on substance and being over against the Platonic approach. Of course, this is part of the broader shift that is introduced with the words τὸ εἶναι πολλαχῶς since potentiality and actuality are two of the general senses of 'being' given elsewhere; cf. *Met.* E 2, 1026b1–2. Thus Aristotle is able to distinguish those things that are prior with respect to potency (τὰ μὲν . . . κατὰ δύναμιν πρότερα ἐστι) from those things that are prior with respect to actuality (κατ' ἐντελέχειαν); cf. *Met.*1019a7–8. For instance, with respect to potency, the half line is prior to the whole line, just as the part (τὸ μόριον) is prior to the whole (τοῦ ὅλου) or as matter (ἡ ὕλη) is prior to substance (τῆς οὐσίας). With respect to actuality, however, the order of priority amongst these things is reversed because the part is really posterior to the whole, just as matter is posterior to substantial form in reality.

This familiar Aristotelian ordering of things looks fairly straightforward until we examine the reason he gives for reversing the order of priority with respect to actuality. Presumably referring to the materials parts, he explains that it is only when the whole is dissolved that they will *be* in actuality.[73] Commentators like Ross[74] and Kirwan[75] have already noted that this explanation poses a difficulty for understanding what Aristotle means by saying that parts are posterior to wholes with respect to actuality (κατ' ἐντελέχειαν δ' ὕστερον) or that matter is posterior to substance in a similar way. In the absence of evidence to the contrary, we must assume that he is still applying the criterion of priority with respect to nature and substance; i.e. whatever can 'exist' without the others is prior, whereas what cannot 'exist' without the others is posterior. But since parts can survive the dissolution of the whole, just as matter can be without substantial form, it would seem that material parts can be naturally or substantially prior to the unified whole. Perhaps it was this rather surprising result that forced Aristotle to make the further distinction between the prior and the posterior with respect to potency and actuality. As Kirwan points out, there are parallel passages in the *Physics* (250a24–25) where he says that when the whole exists, the parts exist only potentially. Similarly, in *Metaphysics* Zeta 10, Aristotle says that the parts into which something is divided as matter (i.e. the material parts) are posterior, whereas those parts that belong to the substance according to its definition are prior; cf. 1035b11–12. Thus it is clear that he is talking about priority in substance when he goes on to say that the soul and its parts are prior to the concrete living thing, whereas the body and its parts are posterior; cf. *Met.*1035b14–22. For instance, if a finger is severed from a living hand, it continues to 'exist' in a certain sense but not as a living finger. As Aristotle puts it, the dead 'finger' continues to be a finger only in name; cf. *Met.*1035b24–25.

Now it is from a similar combination of passages that Kirwan generates his rather artificial version of the interpretive difficulty about material parts being said to be posterior to substantive wholes with respect to actuality. He thinks that "posterior" cannot mean "after" at the end of Delta 11, in spite of the temporal force of the participle διαλυθέντος because this would make some parts both prior and posterior with respect to actuality. Furthermore, he argues, the criterion for such posteriority dictates that material parts "cannot exist without" the substantial whole and this is incompatible with the fact that such parts can exist *after* the whole is dissolved. But even though he is aware that 'being' has many senses, I think that Kirwan may have been misled by his own argument into thinking that 'existence' is univocal. It is possible for Aristotle to claim that the material parts of a living whole cannot 'be' (in the sense of having substantial form) without the whole and, hence, that they are posterior in this sense of actuality. But when the whole is dissolved, they are actualized *as* material parts (which is a different sense of 'being'). Thus, contrary to Kirwan, I do not find inconsistency in Aristotle's two claims that material parts can be actualized through dissolution *and* that they are posterior to the substantial whole with respect to actuality. The point is that, *after* the dissolution of the whole, the material parts will no longer be the matter of *that* substance; just as the severed finger is no longer informed by the life principle that is called ψυχή. So, in spite of what Kirwan claims, it does not follow that material parts would be both prior and posterior "in respect of complete reality" (κατ᾽ ἐντελέχειαν). In this passage Aristotle does not say that material parts are prior in actuality, and Kirwan does not offer a convincing argument for committing him to such a position.[76] Furthermore, even if being posterior in actuality (i.e. in substance) means that material parts "cannot exist without" substantial form, this is not incompatible with "can exist after" because 'existence' (or being) has many senses. The trouble with using "existence" as a translation of τὸ εἶναι is that it gives a false impression of univocity and thus tends to mislead us in interpreting Aristotle. It is for this reason that I prefer to talk about 'being' and 'modes of being' rather than 'existence.'[77]

I think this is also important to keep in mind when we are trying to make sense of Aristotle's puzzling attempt at the end of Delta 11 to reduce all the senses of priority to one general sense:

Indeed, in some sense all objects which are said to be prior and posterior are called so according to these last senses; for with respect to generation some objects can exist without others, such as the whole without the parts, and with respect to destruction it is otherwise, such as the part without the whole. Similarly with the rest.[78]

The first obstacle to understanding this attempted reduction is the difficulty of identifying what Aristotle is referring to when he talks about "these last senses" (ταῦτα). As his translation suggests, Apostle[79] takes the referent to be priority with respect to potentiality and actuality. But Ross[80] thinks that this cannot be the case because all the meanings of 'prior' and 'posterior' are not reducible to these general senses of priority. In his search for a verbal clue to the reduction, he looks instead to the subsequent explanation and finds it in the words ἐνδέχεται ἄνευ τῶν ἑτέρων εἶναι, which contain definite echoes of the criterion of priority with respect to nature and substance.[81] But, in spite of such linguistic evidence, it is still possible to interpret this passage as saying that in a certain way (τρόπον ... τινα) all the meanings of priority may be expressed in terms of priority with respect to potentiality and actuality. For instance, priority with respect to time is reducible to priority with respect to substance, but in order to render this intelligible, one must draw on the distinction between potentiality and actuality. Since this distinction is applicable to each of the categories, it can cover senses like priority in time that are not reducible in a straightforward way to priority in substance. For instance, some things that are prior in time (like the child to the man) are not prior in substance but are prior in potentiality; whereas other things (like the father to the child) are both prior in substance and in actuality. Similarly, the material parts of something may be prior in potentiality to the whole, whereas the substantial whole is prior in actuality to its material parts. The fact that Aristotle uses the part/whole example to illustrate his attempted reduction could also mean that he has in mind priority with respect to potentiality and actuality. If one gives any weight to authority, I think it is significant that Alexander[82] leans toward this interpretation. Furthermore, in his extended treatment of priority with respect to potentiality and actuality at *Metaphysics* Theta 8, Aristotle tries to show how this general sense can cover the other major senses of priority. But since the character of the reduction cannot be decided on the basis of brief and enigmatic remarks in Delta 11, I will postpone any decision on the question to my next chapter, which explores the different senses of priority according to actuality and potentiality.

Conclusion

In this chapter I have surveyed the list of senses of priority given by Aristotle in *Metaphysics* Delta 11, which clearly represents not merely an expansion upon the list given in the *Categories* but also a significant development in his thinking about priority and posteriority. For instance, the conceptual opposition with 'simultaneous' has now disappeared and prior/posterior remain as opposites. In terms of the list itself, we find a great expansion upon the group of meanings determined with reference to a principle beyond the single meaning (i.e. priority in time) given in the *Categories*. Furthermore, while the Platonic sense of priority with respect to nature and substance is recorded in Delta, its guiding criterion is now cleverly adapted to yield an Aristotelian conclusion; i.e. that the primary subject of predication is prior in substance. We recall that any such conclusion was conspicuously absent from the treatment of priority in the *Categories,* even though we should expect to find it there. Another obvious point of contrast is that the principal meaning of priority is no longer identified with time but now it hovers around substance as actuality. Thus, in general, we can trace some clear lines of development toward metaphysical positions that are identifiable as typically Aristotelian. For instance, we find some evidence in Delta 11 that Aristotle is beginning to reject the primacy the Academy gave to mathematical form in favor of biological form as a superior conception of sensible substance.

4

The Focal Sense of Priority

IN THIS CHAPTER I PROPOSE TO PURSUE THE FASCINATING HINT GIVEN AT THE END of Delta 11 that Aristotle considers the many senses of priority to be somehow reducible to one central meaning. As we have seen, however, it is very difficult to decide whether he has in mind priority with respect to substance or priority with respect to potentiality and actuality. Despite tantalizing hints in Delta 11, we are not given sufficient information to make such a decision, and therefore, we must turn for guidance to *Metaphysics* Theta 8, which contains an extended discussion of the different ways in which actuality is prior to potency. Through a careful scrutiny of this discussion, perhaps we can ascertain the precise relationship between priority in actuality and priority in substance, so that we can decide to which sense Aristotle intended to give primacy. Along with helping us to decide this question, the whole chapter has its own intrinsic interest as an elucidation of mature[1] Aristotelian views on substance, actuality, and priority. This will provide an ideal introduction to my last chapter, which discusses the central role of priority in Aristotle's mature metaphysical thinking. In conformity with my usual procedure, let me begin with a fairly literal translation of the Greek text.

Translation of *Metaphysics* Theta 8

Since the many senses of priority have been distinguished, it is obvious that actuality is prior to potentiality. I mean by 'potency' not only the defined sense in which it is said to be the principle of change in another or (in itself) qua other but, generally, every principle of change or rest. For nature is also in the same genus as potency[2] because it is a principle of motion, though not in another but in itself qua itself. Now actuality is prior to all such kinds (of potency) both in definition and in substance, while in one way it is prior in time but in another way not.

Thus it is clear that actuality is prior in definition because that which is capable primarily is capable by virtue of the fact that it may become active. For instance, I call that which is able to build the capacity for building or that which can see (I call) the capacity for seeing or that which can be seen (I call) the visible. And the same account may be given of the others, so that the definition and the knowledge of what is actual must be prior to the definition[3] and knowledge of what is potential.

However, it (i.e. actuality) is prior in time in the following way: while something actual of the same species is prior, yet it is not the same in number. By this I mean that prior in time to this man, who already is in actuality, and to this corn and to this seeing thing, there is matter and seed and the capacity for seeing, which are potentially though not yet actually the man and the corn and the seeing. But prior in time to these there are other things in actuality from which these things came to be. For the actual being that comes to be from some potential being always is (coming to be) by means of some (other) being in actuality; e.g. a man by a man, a musical man by a musical one. There is always something first moving and the mover is already an actuality.

It was said in the accounts concerning substance that everything that is becoming something comes to be from something and by means of something that is also the same in species. Therefore it seems impossible for a builder to be (a builder) unless he has built something or for a lyre player (to be a lyre player) unless he has played the lyre, since whoever learns the lyre does so by playing it and similarly in all other cases. Whence came the sophistical objection that someone not having the science will do what the science involves, since the student does not (yet) have the science. However, on account of the fact that something of what is being generated must (already) have been generated and, generally, of that which is being moved some part has already been moved, as is clear in our inquiries concerning motion, it is perhaps necessary for the learner to have some (part) of the science. Through this argument, therefore, it is clear that actuality is in this way prior to potency, i.e. with respect to generation and with respect to time.

But also, in fact, it is prior in substance because, first, things that are posterior in generation are prior in form and in substance. For instance, the adult is prior to the child and the man to the seed, since the former already has the form whereas the latter does not. And (second) because every generated thing moves toward a principle and a goal, since that-for-the-sake-of-which is a principle and the generation is for the sake of the goal, the actuality is a goal and it is for the sake of this that the potency is acquired. For animals do not see in order to have sight but rather they have sight in order to see. And, similarly, they have the capacity for building in order to build and the capacity for theoretical inquiry in order to speculate. But they do not speculate in order to have the capacity for theoretical inquiry, unless they are students. Yet such people are not engaging in speculation except in a certain sense [or because there is nothing they need speculate about].[4]

Furthermore, matter *is* potentially because it could approach the form but when it *is* actually then it is in the form. Similarly for all the rest and (even) for those whose goal is a motion. Therefore, just as teachers think that the goal has been reached when they are displaying (the student) actually at work, so nature is likewise. If things do not happen thus, it would be like the Hermes of Pauson[5] because, just as in that case, it would be unclear whether the science is inside or outside. For the product is a goal and the actuality is the product. Wherefore the word 'actuality'[6] is used with respect to the product and it suggests completion.

Even though in some cases the exercise[7] is the ultimate end, e.g. of sight, it is seeing and no product[8] other than and apart from it comes to be from sight; whereas in other cases something comes to be from other things, e.g. from housebuilding comes a house apart from the activity of housebuilding; yet in the first case there is nonetheless a goal, while in the second case the goal of the potency is more.[9] For the activity of building is in the thing being built and comes to be simultaneously with it and is in the house. Therefore, in cases where something else is generated besides the exercise (of a capacity), the actuality is in the thing being made; e.g. the actuality of building is in the thing being built, and weaving is in the thing being woven, and similarly for all the others. And, generally, the change is in the thing being changed. But in the case of things for which the product is not different from the activity, in these things themselves belongs the activity; e.g. the seeing is in that which sees, and the speculation is in those who speculate, and the living is in the soul. And this is why happiness (has activity in itself); for it is a certain kind of living. Thus it is clear that the substance or the form is an actuality. According to this argument, it is obvious that actuality is prior in substance to potency, and as we said, in time one actuality always precedes another until the (actuality of the) eternally and primarily moving thing.

But, indeed, (actuality is prior to potency) in a stricter sense because eternal things are prior in substance to destructible things, while nothing in potency is eternal. An argument is this: Every potency is simultaneously (a potency) for contradiction. For, while that which cannot belong could never belong to anything, everything that is capable of being might not be in actuality. Therefore, what is capable of being may either be or not be, so that the same thing is capable of being and of not being. And that which has the capacity for not-being may not be. But that which has the possibility for not-being is destructible, either absolutely or in the same way in which it is held possible for it not to be; i.e. either with respect to place or quantity or quality, or with respect to substance when (it is said) absolutely.

Hence, none of the things that are absolutely indestructible is in potency without qualification, although nothing prevents them from being so in some respect; e.g. with respect to quality or place. Therefore all these things are in activity. Nor are any of the beings that are by necessity (in potency), since these are primary things and if these were not (always) nothing else would be. Nor is motion (in potency) if it is something eternal.[10] Nor, if there is something moved eternally, can it be something moved with respect to potency, except from place to place, and nothing prevents there being matter for this. Wherefore, the sun and the stars and the whole universe are always active and one ought not to fear that any of them will ever stand still, as is feared by those who inquire about nature. Now they (i.e. the heavenly bodies) do not weary of this journeying, since the motion does not belong to them as it does to corruptible things on account of a capacity for opposites, such that the continuance of the motion would be wearisome. For the cause of this (weariness) is substance as matter and potency but not as activity.

But the indestructible things are imitated by things in change, such as earth and fire. The fact is that these are always active, since through themselves and in themselves they have motion. But the other powers, from which these are distinguished, are all of them potencies for contradiction because that which is capable of moving thus is also capable of not moving thus when these are rational potencies. On the other hand, when they are nonrational potencies they will be the same (as rational potencies) by virtue of being present or absent.

If, therefore, there are some such natures or substances as those people talk about in their accounts of ideas, there would be something much more scientific than Science Itself and also something more moved than Motion Itself. For the former would be activities to a greater degree, while the latter would be potencies for them.

It is evident then that activity is prior to potency and to every principle of change.

The Priority of Actuality in Definition and in Time

The chapter begins with an unmistakable reference back to Delta 11 for the many senses of priority (τὸ πρότερον διώρισται ποσαχῶς λέγεται) and then makes the general claim that actuality is obviously prior to potentiality (φανερὸν ὅτι πρότερον ἐνέργεια δυνάμεώς ἐστιν). I think we should treat this claim as being part of the reduction heralded in that passage, since the only exception noted is that of potentiality being prior in time to actuality in a certain way. In line with the generality of his claim, Aristotle insists that he is not confining the meaning of "potentiality" to the special sense applicable to a principle of change (ἀρχὴ μεταβλητική) in something else or in the same thing qua other.[11] Instead, he intends it to cover every principle of change and rest, including nature, which is a kind of potentiality in the sense that it is a moving principle in the same thing qua itself; cf. 1049b8–10. Having established this general sense of potentiality, he now claims that actuality is prior in definition (λόγῳ) and in substance (τῇ οὐσίᾳ) without qualification, whereas in time (χρόνῳ) it is prior in one sense but not in another. After making this general claim, Aristotle proceeds to elucidate these three major senses of priority in ways that are sometimes familiar from previous treatments and sometimes not. In the interests of brevity, let me concentrate upon the new elements.

The terms in which he explains priority in definition suggest that this is a different sense from that which I called "priority in account" with reference to Delta 11. First, the examples given are quite different. In this case, the illustrations emphasize the linguistic fact that a potentiality for seeing or doing is defined in terms of the activity. For instance, we describe the capacity for housebuilding with reference to the activity of building houses, just as we define the capacity for seeing in terms of the corresponding activity. Second, the crucial difference is that this kind of priority in definition is directly linked to priority in knowledge when Aristotle concludes that the definition and/or knowledge of what is potential presupposes the same of what is actual; cf. *Met.* 1049b16–17. In other words, if we wish to know or to define a capacity for doing something, we must look to the definition or the knowledge of the activity itself. Unlike the sort of priority in account that we met in Delta 11, this kind of priority in definition has direct metaphysical implications, as we can see by looking under priority in substance here in Theta 8.

But, first, let us consider the way in which actuality is prior in time to potentiality, since this introduces the teleological perspective that seems to be missing from the treatments of priority with respect to time in both the *Categories* and *Metaphysics* Delta.[12] In our ordinary temporal experience the stage in which an individual is a child comes before the stage in which he or she is a mature adult. This is the way in which what is potential (i.e. the child) is prior in time to what is actual (i.e. the mature adult). But even within ordinary experience, this order of priorities is reversed when we ask about the moving cause of the child. For Aristotle, this turns out to be a grown man who impregnates the woman and so sets the process in motion whose completion is another mature adult of the same kind. It is in terms of examples like these that he draws his general conclusion that it is always through the agency of some actual being (ὑπὸ ἐνεργείᾳ ὄντος) that another thing comes to be an actual being from the state of being potential (ἐκ τοῦ δυνάμει ὄντος); cf. Met.1049b24–25. Another way of formulating the same point (which Aristotle does not use here), is to say that nature in the sense of actuality (i.e. as substantial form) is prior in time to nature in the sense of potentiality (i.e. as matter). What Aristotle does emphasize is that there is always a prime mover (κινοῦντός τινος πρώτου) that already exists in actuality. In terms of natural generation, this prime mover cannot be exclusively identified with any individual animal, even though they are each in their turn actual movers. Thus, if anything, the species itself remains as an identical prime mover for the generation of different individuals. But, since species are held to be eternal, this goes beyond the terms of reference for priority in time.[13]

It also introduces an apparent paradox about learning a craft or a science that the Megarians seem to have exploited in making an argument for the identity of potency and activity. Given that Aristotle has already discussed the absurd implications of such an argument in Theta 3, it is likely that the reference to a sophistical refutation (σοφιστικὸς ἔλεγχος) is aimed at the Megarians.[14] For him one of the most implausible consequences of their view is that there will be no motion or generation because there is no distinction between potency and actuality and hence no transition between one and the other, which is the essence of change; cf. Met.1047a14ff. With reference to knowledge or skill, the Megarian view implies that there is no gradual process of learning or acquisition, but that in some mysterious way someone starts building and is already a builder or starts doing science and is already a scientist. When they stop building or thinking scientifically, however, they suddenly cease to be builders or scientists just as mysteriously as they began. I think that the Megarian argument is similar in many ways to Meno's paradox about learning, and this may help to explain why Aristotle treats both as sophistical difficulties; cf. An.Pst. 71a29ff. His characteristic response to such an impasse is to say that there is a certain way in which we already know what we are learning but there is another way in which we do not, and so there is a genuine process of learning a science or of acquiring a skill. In other words, the learner already possesses some part of the science or the skill, even though the potency for learning is not yet exhausted. Thus, unlike the Megarians, Aristotle can give primacy both in time and in generation to activity without denying the essential function of potency.

The Priority in Substance of Actuality

It should come as no surprise when Aristotle insists that actuality is prior in substance (τῇ οὐσίᾳ) to potentiality, since the paradigm case of actuality is substantial form.[15] Furthermore, in the course of dealing with priority in time, he refers back to his previous discussion of substance in Zeta for the conclusion that everything being generated is being generated *from* something and also *by* something that is the same in species as what will be generated; cf. *Met.*1049b27–29.[16] This conclusion now becomes relevant for understanding the formula that Aristotle gives for priority in substance: i.e. things that are posterior in generation are prior in form or in substance.[17] The examples show clearly what he has in mind when he says that an adult is prior to a child, while a man is also prior to sperm. In case there should be any misunderstanding, he explains that the former in each case already has the form (ἤδη ἔχει τὸ εἶδος) whereas the latter does not yet have it; cf. *Met.*1050a6–7. If we leave out of account the external mover (e.g. the father in relation to the child), the teleological perspective emerges more clearly.[18] Viewing the seed in the process of its development through the embryo stage and then through the postnatal stage, we can say that it is prior in time to the mature adult but posterior in substance. As Aristotle puts it, everything that is being generated proceeds toward a principle and an end.[19]

Reversing our usual assumptions about the temporal direction of causality, he insists that 'that-for-the-sake-of-which' (τὸ οὗ ἕνεκα) is a principle and that generation is guided by some goal; cf. *Met.*1050a8–9. But the goal itself is an actuality (ἐνέργεια) in the sense that the mature adult has complete possession of the substantial form. In comparison with this, the previous stages of development may be described in terms of potentiality (δύναμις), since they are assumed to exist for the sake of reaching this goal; cf. *Met.*1050a9–10. For instance, as Aristotle says, animals have the capacity for sight in order to see and not vice versa. From this teleological perspective on generated things, it is easy to see why he claims that actuality is prior in substance to potentiality. It might be taken as a variation upon his more famous claim that 'nature does nothing in vain.'[20] With reference to human activity we could take this to mean that such natural faculties as the capacity for speculation are for the sake of engaging in theoretical inquiry. Only in the case of students, according to Aristotle, do we find this natural ordering reversed, yet the reversal is merely apparent because they are not speculating in the strict sense. Presumably, he means that students are not moved to speculate out of a natural sense of wonder but rather out of a desire to develop the capacity for theoretical inquiry.

A further argument for making actuality prior in substance is formulated by Aristotle in terms of his ubiquitous distinction between matter and form. He claims that matter 'exists' potentially precisely because it can approach the form ($\tau\grave{o}$ $\epsilon\hat{i}\delta o\varsigma$) and when it has reached the form then it is in actuality; cf. *Met*.1050a15–16. This claim brings out the clear correspondence in Aristotle's thought between the twin distinctions of matter/form and potency/activity.[21] While such correspondence seems particularly appropriate to his account of substantial generation, he also holds that other kinds of change can be expressed in terms of the transition from potency to activity.[22] In fact, he insists that this is so even in cases where the goal is itself a motion. What Aristotle seems to have in mind here is the distinction between activities whose goal is achieved in the production of something external and those whose goal is somehow contained in each activity.[23] An example of the first kind of activity is housebuilding, whose goal is the production of a house that can therefore be said to contain the activity of the housebuilder. By contrast, the second kind of activity is illustrated by vision that has no goal other than its own exercise, just as speculation has no goal other than the activity itself. In both cases, however, the activity is prior to the potency in the sense that it is for the sake of the goal (whether this be a completed house or actually seeing) that the capacity 'exists.'

This priority is illustrated for nature in terms of the example of teachers who consider that they have reached their goal when they are displaying their students at work. Like nature, they are thereby showing that they are not working in vain and that they are not in the situation of Pauson, whose Hermes appeared to be incomplete. For Aristotle, in fact, the conceptual relationship between work and a goal is so close that he gives an etymological derivation of 'activity' ($\dot{\epsilon}v\acute{\epsilon}\rho\gamma\epsilon\iota\alpha$) from 'work' ($\ddot{\epsilon}\rho\gamma ov$) that parallels that of 'actualization' ($\dot{\epsilon}v\tau\epsilon\lambda\acute{\epsilon}\chi\epsilon\iota\alpha$) from 'goal' ($\tau\acute{\epsilon}\lambda o\varsigma$); cf. *Met*.1050a21–23. What the Greek language is made to show here is the intrinsic connection between all work, whether natural or artificial, and some goal in which it finds realization. Aristotle would insist that this is the case even for those activities like seeing and thinking that do not yield some external product and thus do not have any goal beyond themselves. In fact, it is precisely such activities that represent for him the highest realization of the human potential in what have been traditionally called the 'liberal arts.' I suspect that some such line of thought is responsible for happiness being mentioned in this context, since it is associated with the highest activity of the human soul as the form of the body.[24] But within Aristotle's teleological framework the goal is dictated by the form of something rather than by its matter, so it is natural for him to insist that the substance or the form is an activity; cf. *Met.*1050b2. Therefore, by way of conclusion to this long argument, he says it is obvious that activity is prior in substance to potency. With respect to time also, he reminds us that one activity continually precedes another until the regress comes to an end with something first that is eternally moving. This directs our attention toward the cosmological and metaphysical implications of the substantial priority of activity over potency.

The Paradigmatic Sense of Activity

Having drawn attention to the need to halt a possible infinite regress by positing some entity that is eternally moving, Aristotle adverts to a stricter sense (κυριωτέρως)[25] in which activity is prior to potency and by way of explanation says that eternal things are prior in substance (τῇ οὐσίᾳ) to destructible things. In addition, he points out that nothing in potency is eternal and defends the claim with a carefully constructed argument as follows.[26] Every potency is simultaneously a capacity for contradictories because it means that something may or may not 'be,' under whatever genus of being we are talking about. For instance, under the category of substance, potency means that something is capable of being generated and of being destroyed. With one exception, therefore, nothing that has potency is eternal because it is also possible for it not to be either absolutely (with reference to substance) or in some qualified sense (with reference to other categories). The exception is of great interest because it concerns the eternal motion of the heavenly bodies, which seems to presuppose a potency for motion with respect to place. Aristotle insists that such a potency can belong to these bodies because it does not imply destructibility as does potency in the unqualified (ἁπλῶς) sense. Therefore, he concludes, all these things are in activity (ἐνεργείᾳ); cf. *Met.*1050b18.

The cosmological implications of this conclusion become even clearer in the subsequent passage where Aristotle denies that things that exist of necessity (ἐξ ἀνάγκης) have potency in an absolute sense. Their lack of such potency is elucidated, interestingly enough, in terms of their priority and the resultant dependence of other things upon their continual activity. Even the necessity for motion to be eternal excludes it from being potential in an unqualified sense because that would mean that all motion in the universe could cease at some time or other. It is precisely such a traditional fear of the natural philosophers that Aristotle wants to assuage when he argues that the heavenly bodies and indeed the whole universe are eternally active (ἀεὶ ἐνεργεῖ); cf. 1050b22ff. There is a touch of poetic lyricism in his insistence that such bodies do not weary of their journeying because (circular) locomotion does not belong to them on account of a capacity for opposites, as is the case with destructible things that cannot have unceasing motion. The weariness that we experience as a result of continued motion Aristotle attributes to our substance as matter and potency rather than as activity. Behind this explanation lies his assumption of a radical division between terrestrial and celestial things, which roughly corresponds to the traditional Greek dichotomy between divine and human things.

In fact, I think that some such dichotomy provides the essential framework for understanding Aristotle's implicit connection between actuality in the stricter sense and the primary sense of substance. The fact that he makes substance as matter responsible for the cessation of motion implies that substance as form is the cause of continuing motion. Thus, if there were a pure form that was separated from all potency, it would presumably be the source of eternal activity. This is not stated explicitly by Aristotle in Theta 8, but I think that there is some evidence for such a train of thought. Near the end of the chapter, for example, he says that if there are such natures or substances (οὐσίαι) as those posited by the Platonists, then these would be more scientific (μᾶλλον ἐπιστῆμον) than science itself because they would be greater actualities (ἐνέργειαι μᾶλλον) than the latter that are merely potencies for them. While this might be interpreted as being a purely negative critique, I think the context suggests that Aristotle wishes to draw some positive conclusions about the sort of substance that would be separate from and independent of sensible things. For instance, such eternal things would be prior in substance to destructible things and, consequently, would also be prior in actuality to entities that have the potency for generation and destruction. But there is little evidence in Theta 8 that Aristotle was thinking explicitly of the Prime Mover as a pure activity without any potency even for circular motion.[27] Indeed, there is some evidence that he still thinks of the heavenly bodies as being self-moved when he says that such indestructible things are imitated by elemental bodies like earth and fire, which are always active (ἀεὶ ἐνεργεῖ) because they are self-moved; cf. *Met.*1050b28–30. However we interpret such a statement, it does not suggest that Aristotle is looking beyond the heavenly bodies to the Prime

Mover as a source of their eternal motion. This is a further step connected with another argument from priority that I will consider in my final chapter.[28]

Conclusion

While *Metaphysics* Theta 8 does not contain Aristotle's final word on every point, it undoubtedly represents his most complete and mature treatment of the different senses of priority. Situated within a treatise on actuality and potency, which are central concepts in his thinking about sensible substance, the chapter establishes the primacy of activity in all of the important senses. It also clears up an ambiguity in Delta 11 by showing that the primacy of activity depends ultimately upon the priority of substance over all the other genera of being. Even within the category of substance, however, there is an ordering that depends upon the degree to which the substantial form is separated from matter and hence from the potency for corruption and change. Since they have such a potency, therefore, living things in the sublunary sphere are inferior in substance to the heavenly bodies that have merely a potency for eternal and circular locomotion. Though we do not find it explicit in Theta 8, we can see how such a hierarchy of substances points toward the Prime Mover as a pure activity that is without any potency whatsoever. This also tends to confirm our suspicion that some version of a degrees-of-being thesis is an integral part of Aristotle's mature metaphysical thought.

5

Getting the Priorities Right

HAVING DEVOTED SO MUCH TIME TO REVIEWING THE DIFFERENT SENSES OF priority, it is now time to show the importance of this notion in some central passages from Aristotle's *Metaphysics*. This will complete my attempt at proving that the thesis about the many senses of 'priority' is equally important for understanding his metaphysical positions as the more famous claim that 'being' is said in many ways. In fact, I will begin with a passage from *Metaphysics* Zeta, where the two concepts are clearly interdependent. Aristotle introduces this book with the claim about the many senses of being and proceeds to outline his own categories. If we follow his reference back to a previous treatise "On the many senses" (περὶ τοῦ ποσαχῶς), we find at *Metaphysics* Delta 7 that the categorical uses of 'being' form only one of the major senses along with truth, actuality and potentiality, and accident. In Zeta 1, however, he concentrates upon outlining the senses of being according to the categories, while insisting that the primary being is the what-it-is that refers to substance.[1] The key to understanding the primacy of the "whatness" (τὸ τί ἐστι) lies in the categorical framework according to which it provides the appropriate answer to the first question (i.e. What is it?) about some particular thing. Incidentally, the primacy of this question that leads to definition is perhaps *the* fundamental assumption of the whole Academic tradition that traces its origins to Socrates.[2] Thus, drawing once more on the terminology of the *Topics,* one can say that the whatness is prior by nature (πρότερον τῇ φύσει) and more intelligible absolutely (γνωριμώτερον ἁπλῶς), although it is no longer identified with the more universal genera that are assumed by Plato to be prior and more intelligible in these senses. Toward the end of the chapter, I shall examine some of the implications of this break with Platonism for the question about the ontological status of mathematical objects.

The Universal Priority of Substance

Even though Platonic terminology is not evident in Zeta 1, I think that
the Academic background is important to keep in mind when we are examining Aristotle's claim that substance is prior in every sense. All other categorical predicates, such as quantity, quality, and relation, are held to be secondary beings because they are attributes of that which 'exists' in the
primary sense; cf. *Met.*1028a18–20. Just like walking or sitting or being
healthy, none of these dependent attributes can exist by itself (καθ' αὐτὸ)
nor can it be separated from substance (χωρίζεσθαι ... τῆς οὐτίας); cf.
1028a23–24.[3] Thus Aristotle argues that all categorical predicates other
than substance have a dependent mode of being. While they have being in a
certain sense (τὶ ὄν), substance is the only thing that has being in a sense
that is primary (πρώτως) and absolute (ἀπλῶς); cf. 1028a29–31. At this
point in Zeta 1 we find the following passage:

> Now the term "primary" (or "first" or "prior to all others") is used in many
> senses, yet a substance is primary in every sense: in formula, in knowledge,
> and in time. For of the other categories no one is separable, but only sub-
> stance. And in formula, too, substance is primary; for in the formula of each
> of the other categories the formula of a substance must be present. And we
> think we understand each thing to the highest degree when we know, for ex-
> ample, what a man is or what a fire is, rather than their quality or their quan-
> tity or their whereness, and even of these latter, we understand each when we
> know what a quantity is or what a quality is. And indeed the inquiry or per-
> plexity concerning what being is, in early times and now and always, is just
> this: what is substance?[4]

From the point of view of my argument, it is significant that the thesis
about the many senses of priority is here formulated in exactly the same
terms as the thesis about the multiple senses of being at the beginning of the
chapter. When Aristotle says, quite literally, that "the first is said in many
ways" (πολλαχῶς ... λέγεται τὸ πρῶτον) this suggests that 'priority' is a
pros hen equivocal analogous to 'being.'[5]

Such a suggestion tends to be supported by his consistent attempts (some
of which we have noted) to identify the strictest (κυριώτατος) meaning of
'priority.' But just as in the case of being, one might also take this statement
to be simply a reference back to Delta 11, where the many senses of priority
have been outlined. This reading is supported to a certain extent by what he
says about substance, namely, that it is first in every sense (πάντως).
Aristotle would seem to be presupposing here that his audience, on hearing
the characteristic phrase πολλαχῶς λέγεται, will immediately be reminded

of the complete treatment of priority in Delta 11. Otherwise it is difficult to explain why he seems to claim completeness for the list of meanings given in Zeta 1. Perhaps he is offering a complete list of all the *relevant* senses in which substance is prior when he gives the following: (i) in definition (λόγῳ); (ii) in knowledge (γνώσει); and (iii) in time (χρόνῳ). But this seems to leave out the rather important sense in which substance is prior with respect to actuality (κατ' ἐντελέχειαν).[6] Yet, it may be the case that the list in Zeta 1 is being treated merely as a representative sample of the most important senses of priority that are relevant to substance. If we check these against the comprehensive list in Delta 11, we find that he gives at least one crucial meaning from each of the three clusters that I have identified there. For instance, priority in time is a leading example of priority with reference to some principle, whether determined absolutely or relatively. Furthermore, from the treatment of priority at Theta 8, we can supply the insight that in a certain way substance as actuality is prior in time to potential being; cf. *Met.*1049b17ff. The second major sense of priority is over-represented in Zeta 1 by priority with respect to knowledge and priority with respect to definition, which amount to the same thing if we take 'knowledge' here in the sense of what is more familiar absolutely. Hence Aristotle would appear to be neglecting the third major sense of priority with respect to nature and substance but I think that this appearance is misleading. In the case of substance, all of these senses dovetail so neatly that one is tempted to take this as the focus for the clustering of meanings that constitute his treatments of priority. It should be noted, however, that this impression might result from the related (but conceptually independent) fact that substance is the primary and focal meaning of being.[7]

Whether or not all the different senses of priority are reduced to one, it is clear that Aristotle attaches considerable importance to his explicit claim that substance is prior in every sense. After listing three specific meanings of priority, he briefly outlines a number of different criteria by which one can judge that substance is prior. One puzzling feature of his treatment here is that, while he gives explicit criteria for priority in definition and in knowledge, he appears to neglect priority in time if we interpret this in the usual temporal sense. In view of previous treatments, we would expect some reference to the 'now' as a principle for determining such priority. Instead, we find Aristotle explaining that none of the other categories is separated (χωριστόν) but only substance (αὕτη . . . μόνη); cf. *Met.*1028a33–34.[8] This explanation seems to involve an application of the criterion for priority with respect to nature and substance; cf. *Met.*1019a1–4. But drawing upon the insights of Theta 8 once more, we can see that in the special case of substance this might double as a criterion for priority in time.[9] The word χωριστόν serves to underline the independence and self-subsistence of substance in contrast to the other categories.[10] Thus, for instance, there is an important sense in which there cannot be a quantity or a quality *before* there is a substantial subject for such attributes.[11]

The role of substance as a subject for other predicates is also crucial for understanding the claim that it is prior in definition. Aristotle defends his claim by arguing that the definition of a substance must be present in the definition of each of its dependent predicates; cf. *Met.* 1028a35–36. Now the necessity of this is not immediately obvious, since it seems possible to give a definition of whiteness (e.g. a certain color in a surface) without making any reference to substance. But it would appear that Aristotle has in mind something like the following argument: since a surface depends upon a particular substance, the definition of whiteness that refers to surface also implicitly refers to substance.[12] Still, this claim about the primacy of substance in definition (λόγῳ) cannot be fully understood without a detailed discussion of Zeta 4 and 5, where he says that there can be definition only of something primary (πρώτου τινὸς) like substance but not of such things as are predicated of something else; cf. *Met.*1030a10–11. Even though Aristotle later concedes that of these other predicates we may have definition in a qualified sense, he insists that definition in the absolute sense (ἁπλῶς) as an account of the essence (τὸ τί ἦν εἶναι) applies primarily (πρώτως) to substance (τῇ οὐσίᾳ); cf. *Met.*1030a17–27. The main reason given for this is that the "whatness" (τὸ τί ἐστιν) in its primary sense refers to substance and to a 'this' (τόδε τι); cf. *Met.* 1030a18–19. I think it is sufficiently clear that this discussion in Zeta 4 to 6 provides the appropriate context for understanding the claim that substance is prior in definition.[13]

For further elucidation of this claim we might glance briefly at a related discussion in Zeta 10 to 12, where Aristotle considers the *aporia* about whether or not the definitions of the parts of a thing should be present in the definition of the whole thing that contains these parts. The impasse is generated by an apparent conflict between the fact that the segments of a circle, for instance, are not mentioned in its definition and the fact that the letters of a syllable are. Additional sources for the difficulty are found in different senses of priority. For example, if the parts are assumed to be prior to the whole then it follows that the acute angle is prior to the right angle and the finger is prior to the man; cf. *Met.* 1034b28–30. But on the other hand, it seems that the latter member of each related pair is prior both in definition (τῷ λόγῳ) and in being (τῷ εἶναι) because the first is defined in terms of the second and also cannot 'exist' without it; cf. *Met.*1034b30–32. While Aristotle generates the *aporia* by trading upon different senses of 'priority,' he offers a resolution that depends upon distinguishing in a similar way between different senses of 'part.' If we consider man as a composite (συνόλον) then we could treat his finger as a prior part in the sense of matter (ὡς ὕλη), but such material parts are not present in the account of his substantial form; cf. *Met.* 1035a1–9. This is Aristotle's explanation of why the definition of a circle contains no reference to its segments, even though any account of a syllable does refer to its constituent letters. In a subsequent attempt to clarify his resolution of the guiding *aporia,* he distinguishes the different senses of 'part' from each other in terms of priority relations; cf. *Met.*1035b3ff. While those that are parts of the substantial form are held to be prior, parts into which things are divisible as matter are said to be posterior (presumably in the same sense); cf. *Met.* 1035b11–14. Aristotle does not specify the sense of 'prior' and 'posterior' that he has in mind, but I think one can gather from the context that it is priority and posteriority in definition. Thus the whole passage may be taken to illustrate another way in which substance is prior in definition.

Similarly it is possible to use this same passage to render intelligible the further claim that substance is prior in knowledge. According to the passage quoted above from Zeta 1, substance is prior in knowledge (γνώσει) because we think that we understand each thing to the highest degree (μάλιστα) when we know *what is* a man, for instance, or *what is* fire rather than the quality (τὸ ποιὸν) or the quantity (τὸ ποσὸν) or the location (τὸ πού) of the individual thing. Each of these categories represents an answer to a specific question that one can ask about things (e.g. What sort? How much? Where?), and the priority of substance follows from the priority of the question, What is it? Even in the case of secondary predicates such as quantity and quality, Aristotle claims that we know them better when we grasp *what* they are in a definition. As I have already noted, it is rather strange to find a thesis that originated with Socrates being made the point of departure for Aristotle's break with Platonism.[14] But it should be clear by now that everything depends on how the appropriate criterion of priority is applied. For instance, in the *Topics* and the *Posterior Analytics,* we found that the genus was held to be prior in knowledge to the species because it is prior by nature and more intelligible absolutely. In *Categories* 5, on the other hand, the species (rather than the genus) is said to be more intelligible and more appropriate to give in answer to the what-is-it question about primary substances; cf. *Cat.* 2b7 ff. There the justification is that the species is more peculiar (ἴδιον μᾶλλον) to the particular substance than the genus, which is more general (κοινότερον). I do not see any way to reconcile these conflicting statements other than to say that they involve the application of different criteria of priority, some of which are distinctively Platonic in character. But as I have shown, even the application of the same criterion can yield different results when it is put to work on different concepts. In the *Categories,* for instance, the fundamental assumption is that all the other categorical predicates are dependent on primary substances as subjects, and as far as I can see, the same assumption lies behind the claim in *Metaphysics* Zeta that substance is prior in every sense.[15]

We find an important application of this claim in Zeta 13 when Aristotle turns to the question of whether or not the universal (τὸ καθόλου) is a substance. According to some people (presumably the Platonists), the universal is a cause especially (μάλιστα) and is also a principle (ἀρχή). Since the universal also represents the claims of the genus (τὸ γένος) to be a substance, I think it is plausible to interpret this as the Platonic view about their primacy and greater degree of being. Thus it is particularly appropriate that, among the arguments against accepting the universal as a substance, Aristotle constructs one upon the priority of substance as follows. It is impossible and absurd, he argues, that what is a this and a substance (οὐσ ία) should be composed of parts that are qualities rather than substances or 'thises,' since that would make nonsubstance or quality prior to substance and to a 'this'; cf. *Met.* 1038b23–27. But, he concludes, this is impossible because attributes are not prior to substance either in definition (τῷ λόγῳ) or in time (χρόνῳ) or in generation (γενέσει); otherwise they would be separated (χωριστά).[16]

The impossibility here seems to be that constitutive elements of a substance should be separated from it and hence be prior in any or all of the senses outlined. It is not clear whether each sense of priority implies the separation of substantial constituents or whether that requires all of the senses to be combined. In Delta 11, for instance, we found that the part may be prior to the whole in a certain sense of priority with respect to account, but that this does not imply the separation of the part. And even for the stronger sense of priority in definition, the genus and differentia could be prior to the species without being separated from it. This now puts the burden of separation upon priority in time and in generation, which are not distinguished elsewhere by Aristotle.[17] But if the genus 'animal' is prior in time and in generation to the substance 'man,' it follows that there will be a separate substance, such as a generic animal, that is an individual just like the individual man who is prior in time to the son he generates. Therefore, Aristotle rejects the claims of a universal or of a genus to be substantial because these absurdities will result from it.[18]

Hierarchy among Theoretical Sciences

In order to illustrate the importance of the notion of priority in Aristotle's account of the sciences, let us look briefly at a passage in *Metaphysics* Epsilon 1 that has often puzzled commentators. The chapter is mainly concerned with making distinctions between the three theoretical sciences in terms of their respective subject genera. Unless one can unearth the problems that are being resolved through such distinctions, one might be tempted to view Aristotle as a thinker obsessed with distinctions for their own sake. In this particular case, the only clue to the problem being considered is found in the following passage:

> One might raise the question whether first philosophy is in any way universal or is concerned mainly with some genus and some one nature. In the case of the mathematical sciences, their objects are not all treated in the same manner; geometry and astronomy are concerned with some nature, but universal mathematics is common to all. Accordingly, if there were no substances other than those formed by nature, physics would be the first science; but if there is an unmovable substance, this would be prior, and the science of it would be first philosophy and would be universal in this manner, in view of the fact that it is first. And it would be the concern of this science, too, to investigate being qua being, both what being is and what belongs to it qua being.[19]

The difficulty mentioned at the beginning of this passage is one of the most famous problems in the history of Aristotelian scholarship; namely, whether the science of metaphysics is an inquiry into *all* beings (i.e. metaphysica generalis) or whether, as theology, it is concerned only with "the most honorable genus" (τὸ τιμιώτατον γένος) of beings (i.e. metaphysica specialis).[20] Within the context there appears to be some evidence that Aristotle conceives of this new science as special metaphysics. In a previous passage, for instance, it is distinguished from the other theoretical sciences by virtue of the fact that its objects of study are eternal, immovable, and separate (ἀΐδιον καὶ ἀκίνητον καὶ χωριστόν); cf. *Met.* 1026a10ff. Subsequently, the science is called theology (θεολογική) because it is most appropriate for the divine (τὸ θεῖον) to be present in things of such a nature; cf. *Met.* 1026a18–22. Yet all of this evidence does not clinch the matter because it is precisely at this point that Aristotle raises the difficulty. In addition, the description of his projected science of being qua being in *Metaphysics* Gamma 1 clearly states that it studies things in a universal manner, by contrast with the particular interests of the special sciences; cf. *Met.* 1003a21ff. I take it that this is what he means by the first option in the above *aporia;* i.e. whether first philosophy is in any way universal.[21] The second option is that this science is concerned with a particular genus and with some one nature (περί τι γένος καὶ φύσιν τινὰ μίαν); i.e. the divine. It would appear that these are equally plausible options that are mutually exclusive, and that as a result, we have reached an impasse in thought.[22]

Aristotle's sketch of a solution to this impasse is so brief as to be enigmatic. For one thing, it is not entirely clear what he means to achieve through the comparison with the mathematical sciences.[23] On the face of it, this parenthetical comparison seems intended merely to illustrate the difference between the two options in the *aporia*. For instance, if first philosophy is a special science then it will be like geometry and astronomy, which are each concerned with some particular nature (περί τινα φύσιν). But, on the other hand, if it is in any way universal, it will be more like universal mathematics, which is about something common to all these particular natures (ἡ δὲ καθόλου πασῶν κοινή); i.e. quantity. What is unclear is whether or not the comparison with universal mathematics is intended to point us toward a solution to the impasse.[24] Without clarifying the comparison, Aristotle proceeds to set out two other mutually exclusive options that are formulated hypothetically as follows: (A) If there were no other substance apart from those constituted by nature (τὰς φύσει συνεστηκυίας) then physics would be the first science (φυσικὴ ἂν εἴη πρώτη ἐπιστήμη); but (B) if there is some changeless substance (εἰ δ' ἔστι τις οὐσία ἀκίνητος) this will be prior (αὕτη προτέρα) and the science of it will be first philosophy. Clearly, the first step toward a solution is to choose the subject matter of first philosophy from the two options set out in the above conditional statements. The decision hangs on the crucial question of whether or not there is some unchanging substance apart from natural substances. If not, then physics will be identical with first philosophy. But if there is such a substance then, according to Aristotle, it will be prior to natural substances and will be the subject of *first* philosophy, as the name of that science suggests.[25] Furthermore, as he goes on to explain, this science will be universal in a certain way precisely because it is primary (καὶ καθόλου οὕτως ὅτι πρώτη).

In spite of its explicitness, this explanation is far from clear.[26] What is fairly clear from the context is that it represents an attempt on the part of Aristotle to resolve the initial impasse about whether first philosophy is universal in any way or whether it is exclusively about some particular genus. At first glance, however, the solution seems inconsistent because it tries to unite what were previously outlined as two mutually exclusive options; i.e. that first philosophy is about a particular kind of substance (i.e. unchanging and separate) and that this science is universal in some way.[27] In order to make sense of this 'solution,' one must try to determine more exactly what sense of "universal" is compatible with first philosophy having a particular kind of subject matter. Since it cannot mean 'universal' in the sense of a whole that encompasses all the parts (ὡς περιέχουσα), Alexander[28] thinks an appropriate sense might be that applied to universal things that are more praiseworthy (τὸ τιμιώτερα) and more choiceworthy (αἱρετώτερα). It is no coincidence, I think, that this corresponds to the estranged sense of priority which we noted in the *Categories*, i.e. that what is better (τὸ βέλτιον) and more honorable (τὸ τιμιώτερον) is thought to be prior by nature (τῇ φύσει); cf. 14b4–5. Obviously this would be an appropriate sense in which one could say that the divine is prior and perhaps Aristotle is here drawing on ordinary speech. Furthermore, if Alexander is correct about the related sense of 'universal,' we can understand how Aristotle can argue from the priority of first philosophy (as an inquiry about the highest things) to its universality. But in order to confirm such an interpretation, we should be able to find the term 'universal' being used by Aristotle in this special sense. Since there is no more help to be found in *Metaphysics* Epsilon, perhaps we should follow the direction in which it points toward Gamma and briefly explore the relationship between priority and the concept of *pros hen* equivocal as explored in that book.

By contrast with the conditional statements of Epsilon, Book Gamma begins with the categorical assertion that there is some science of being qua being (ὂν ᾖ ὄν) and of its *per se* attributes. But, just as in Epsilon, this science is differentiated from the so-called partial sciences by virtue of the fact that they consider only some particular genus of being and do not inquire universally (καθόλου) about being qua being. While we might take this to be a methodological distinction between general and particular sciences, I think it would be more consistent with Aristotle's approach to interpret the distinction as depending upon differences in their respective objects. In this regard we should note that he cites the mathematical sciences as examples of the particular sciences, and we know that he differentiates these from physics in terms of their characteristic objects rather than in terms of their method. Against this background it is significant that, from the fact that "we" seek the principles and the highest causes (ἀκρόταται αἰτίαι), he argues in Gamma 1 to the existence of some particular nature (φύσις τις) to which they belong *per se;* cf. *Met.* 1003a26–28. Furthermore, if these principles are identical with the so-called elements (στοιχεῖα) sought by other thinkers, he claims that they must also be the elements of being qua being. Thus Aristotle concludes his introduction to Gamma by identifying his project as the search for the first causes of being qua being. It is difficult to escape the impression that he is talking about a particular subject matter, even though he insists that it is not like that of the special sciences.

Although Aristotle does not advert here to the *aporia* of Epsilon about whether the subject matter of wisdom is particular or universal, one might plausibly assume that he is aware of the problem in Gamma and is trying to resolve it. Indeed, it is arguable that the first step toward this resolution is taken when he declares that being is said in many senses but, especially, with reference to some one single nature (πρὸς ἓν καὶ μίαν τινὰ φύσιν); cf. *Met.* 1003a32ff. Thus he claims that 'being' is not spoken of homonymously but rather in the way that all healthy things are so named with reference to health in a living thing or the way in which all uses of 'medical' are referring ultimately to the medical art. Similarly, 'being' is said in many ways but all of these senses refer to a single principle (πρὸς μίαν ἀρχήν) that is substance. Hence things are called 'beings' in the primary and strictest sense precisely because they are substances, while everything else is called this in a secondary and derivative sense because of some relation that it has to substance; cf. *Met.* 1003b6ff.

This logical (and ontological) fact about 'being' is now used by Aristotle to justify the possibility of a single science of wisdom, even though 'being' itself is not a genus; cf. *Met.* 1003b11ff. He begins by making a comparison with 'health,' which has a similar equivocal structure and yet there is a single science of all healthy things. The reason for this, according to Aristotle, is that it is possible to have a single science not only of things that are spoken of according to one nature (καθ' ἕν) but also of things said in relation to one nature (πρὸς μίαν φύσιν); cf. *Met.* 1003b12–14. If the first possibility corresponds to his standard view that each science has only one genus of things as its subject matter, then we might be forgiven for assuming that the second possibility is incompatible with that view, since it envisages a single science that studies things from many different genera. But Aristotle undermines that assumption by claiming that things spoken of with reference to one nature are also in some way (τρόπον τινὰ) said according to one nature; cf. *Met.* 1003b14–15. Thus he concludes that there is obviously a single theoretical inquiry about being qua beings.

In spite of such definite conclusions, however, the traditional problem lingers in our minds as to whether this science is about *ens commune* or *ens perfectissimum,* as the Schoolmen put it. While there is little evidence that Aristotle addresses this problem in Gamma, perhaps we can find some passages that show why such a problem might not be insuperably difficult for him to resolve. For instance, immediately after reaching the conclusion that there is a single science of being qua being, he makes the following remarks presumably by way of elaboration:

> In every case the fundamental concern of a discipline is with its primary [object], i.e. that on which the others depend and to which they owe their being

called [what they are]. So if this thing is substance, the philosopher will need to have the principles and causes of substances.[29]

As Kirwan notes, this is the first explicit statement in Gamma that substance is prior to all other beings. Yet the important connection between this statement and what has gone before is not sufficiently recognized by commentators.[30] Aristotle has claimed, without any argument or clarification, that the things spoken of *pros hen* are also in some way spoken of *kath hen*. Now, since his conclusion about the existence of a single science of being qua being seems to depend on this claim, I think it is unlikely that he would leave it without some defense or justification. In fact, such a justification can be found in the argument of the above passage when it is viewed from this perspective.

The initial assertion puts wisdom in the same boat as the other sciences because, strictly speaking (κυρίως), science inquires about what is first (τοῦ πρώτου). Aristotle then appeals to two different criteria of priority as (i) that on which the others depend (ἐξ οὗ τὰ ἄλλα ἤρτηται) and as (ii) that because of which they are spoken about (δι' ὃ λέγονται).[31] But as we have seen in Zeta 1, both criteria are satisfied by substance that is prior in all of the relevant senses. Therefore, Aristotle concludes, since substance is prior in the strictest sense, the philosopher needs to grasp the principles and the causes of substances. Within the context of his previous discussion, the implication of this conclusion is that philosophy will study a single genus of being like the other special sciences, while simultaneously considering the whole of being (or being qua being) by virtue of the fact that substance is the primary sense of being as a *pros hen* equivocal. So the brief and enigmatic assertion in Epsilon 1 makes sense when we look to Gamma for elucidation.

Before we leave Gamma 2, however, there is another passage that is relevant to the present topic; i.e. the ordering of the sciences. Directly after his parenthetical discussion of the identity of unity and being, which does not appear to be continued, we find the following:

And there are as many parts of philosophy as there are substances; so that it is necessary that there be among them a first and a next. For that which is divides directly into genera; hence the disciplines too will follow these. For the philosopher is like the mathematician, as he is called; for that also has parts, a primary and a secondary discipline and others successively within mathematics.[32]

This passage shows some of the implications that follow from Aristotle's tendency to differentiate the sciences according to their characteristic objects rather than by their respective methods. For instance, he claims that there are just as many parts of philosophy as there are different kinds of substance. But it is not immediately clear how it follows necessarily that there is among them (i.e. either the parts of philosophy or among substances) something first (πρώτη) and something subsequent (ἐχομένη). Perhaps Aristotle is referring to some categorical ordering when he explains that being is divided into genera, and therefore, that the sciences follow those. But surely this will not fit the comparison he makes between the philosopher and the mathematician, since the latter is concerned exclusively with the category of quantity. The ordering of the sciences within mathematics seems to presuppose some Pythagorean schema of priority like unit, point, line, plane, and solid. If Aristotle is serious about a corresponding ordering among the philosophical sciences then he must mean that, within the category of substance itself, there is a similar way of establishing that one kind of substance is prior and another secondary or posterior. But in Gamma 2 he does not clarify his meaning further and so we must turn to Book Lambda in pursuit of such clarification.

Priority of the Prime Mover

Even though priority plays a role in many of the arguments of Lambda, I will concentrate on a few passages that are also relevant to the impasse about first philosophy raised in Epsilon. Another way of formulating the difficulty is as follows: since this projected science is about causes and principles, it is appropriate to ask whether these are different for different things or the same for all; cf. *Met.* 1070a33ff. If they are different for each genus of things, then it would seem that there can only be particular sciences and no single science that investigates the principles and causes of all things. One of these special sciences might be theology, but it would simply deal with a particular genus of objects that are eternal and unchanging. Thus, like the other special sciences, it would be concerned merely with a part of being and not with the whole. On the other hand, if the principles and causes are in some sense the same for all things, then the possibility of a universal science like Plato's dialectic would be opened up. But it is notorious that Aristotle rejected such a mistress science of reality in its Platonic form,[33] and that rejection would seem to eliminate the possibility of a general metaphysics such as he conceived first philosophy to be. Here we have another version of the impasse at Epsilon 1 yet this time formulated in terms of causes and principles at the beginning of Lambda 4.

Aristotle begins with a characteristic statement to the effect that, in one way (ὥς), the causes and principles of distinct things are different, but that in another way, they are the same for all if one speaks universally and analogically.[34] This statement must be understood with reference to the subsequent *aporia* about whether the principles and elements (ἀρχαὶ καὶ στοιχεῖα) of substances and relations are the same or different; cf. *Met.* 1070a33–35. On the one hand, Aristotle says, it is absurd (ἄτοπον) that they should be the same because that would mean that substances and relations (and beings falling under the other categories) would have to come from the same elements; yet (he maintains) there is nothing common (κοινόν) to all of the categories. Furthermore, even though substance is prior[35] as an element, it is not an element of relative things, nor are any of these relatives an element of substance. Aristotle thus gives a number of reasons along these lines for thinking that all things cannot have the same elements; cf. *Met.* 1070b1–10. But on the other hand, he holds that there is a definite sense in which all things have the same causes and principles when these are characterized generally as form, privation, and matter. It is obviously the universal and analogical sense that Aristotle has in mind when he claims that, in a certain way, the elements and principles of all things are the same; cf. *Met.* 1070b16–18. By way of summary he says that, taken analogically (κατ' ἀναλογίαν), there are three elements (form, privation, and matter) and four causes or principles (when the moving cause is added); cf. *Met.* 1070b25–27. Now this would appear to be a summary of the subject matter for a science of general metaphysics that inquires into the elements and causes of all things, when these are treated in an analogical manner. But analogy presupposes that there is a definite proportion between terms, such as obtains between the form of a sensible substance and the form of a quality like color.[36] For instance, just as substantial form is related to its appropriate matter, so also qualitative form is related to its proper matter. Yet if we try to draw a similar analogy between sensible and supersensible substance, the proportion begins to break down because the Prime Mover, for instance, does not have any appropriate matter nor any state of privation.[37] Once more, this brings us back to the question of whether Aristotle's theology constitutes a special or a general metaphysics.

Let us approach the question from a different direction by briefly considering another sense in which Aristotle says that the principles of all things are the same; i.e. in the sense of actuality and potentiality (οἷον ἐνέργεια καὶ δύναμις); cf. *Met.* 1071a3–5. The elucidation of this sense is explicitly taken up in Lambda 5 as a clear continuation of the previous issue of whether the causes and principles of all things are the same or different.

Just as in the previous chapter, however, he recognizes that principles that are analogically the same may be quite different in distinct genera. The distinction between actuality and potentiality applies differently to cases where the matter of the cause and of the effect is not the same because, in such cases, even the form (τὸ εἶδος) is different. For instance, one can distinguish between the proximate and ultimate causes of a man and these two kinds of cause need not share the same form or matter. Thus, the proximate causes of a man are the constitutive elements (i.e. matter and form) and the external cause (i.e. the father), which has the same form. Yet the ultimate causes (i.e. the sun and its oblique course, according to Aristotle) do not have the same form or matter as man, since they do not belong to the same species, and are movers (κινοῦντα); cf. *Met.* 1071a11–17. Still, he thinks it is possible to talk universally (καθόλου . . . εἰπεῖν) about causes, as long as one avoids the Platonist assumption that there are universal causes (τὰ καθόλου).[38] Aristotle insists that, in the case of particulars (τῶν καθ᾽ ἕκαστον), the primary principles (πρῶται ἀρχαί) are, on the one hand, a primary 'this' existing actually (τὸ ἐνεργείᾳ πρῶτον τοδὶ) and, on the other hand, some other potential thing (καὶ ἄλλο ὃ δυνάμει); cf. *Met.* 1071a18–19.

Here the emphasis upon the primacy with respect to actuality of the particular as a cause of another particular is an important part of his anti-Platonic stance. This comes out even more clearly in the example used: whereas man is the principle of man in a universal sense (καθόλου), it is a particular man like Peleus who is the proximate cause (as father) of an individual such as Achilles; cf. *Met.* 1071a19–21. What Aristotle is explicitly denying here is that the Idea of Man (or the universal man) has a mode of being such that, by existing actually or potentially, it could serve as the proximate cause of individual men. But the implicit challenge to Platonism goes much deeper, as we shall see, when he replaces the Idea of the Good with the Sun and its oblique course and, ultimately, with the Prime Mover. Before we move on to consider the priority involved there, it is important to note the conclusion of Aristotle's inquiry as to whether the principles or elements of all things are the same or different. When one considers the categories of substance, relation, and quality separately, he says, then their principles and elements are obviously different. But there is also a certain sense in which they are the same by analogy (τῷ ἀνάλογον) when we describe them in general terms as matter, form, privation, and moving cause; cf. *Met.* 1071a29ff. Still, this sort of sameness by analogy does not provide adequate foundations for a single science of wisdom that is both universal and particular.

Yet there is another sense in which principles are the same because the causes of substances are the causes of all things.[39] While this sense has been mentioned previously in the discussion, it is not clear that it comes under sameness by analogy.[40] Aristotle seems to be aware that he has not prepared the way for this particular conclusion when he offers the following justification: the causes of substances are the causes of all because when substances are destroyed all other things are destroyed (ὅτι ἀναιρεῖται ἀναιρουμένων); cf. *Met.* 1071a35. By now we should immediately recognize this formulaic phrase from the Academic criterion of priority and not be surprised that Aristotle should apply it here to justify the natural priority of substances. In this light we can begin to make some sense of his further claim that the first thing existing in actuality (τὸ πρῶτον ἐντελεχείᾳ) is the cause of all; cf. *Met.* 1071a36. If we interpret this claim in terms of proximate causes, an application of the criterion of dependence would imply that the principles and elements are the same (in some sense) for an individual man and for his qualities and quantities. But perhaps Aristotle is talking about ultimate causes and thus is pointing to a special sense in which the causes of this first substance are the same for all things. In pursuit of that special sense, let us now briefly examine the kinds of priority associated with the Prime Mover as a first substance.

Aristotle begins his treatment of supersensible substance rather abruptly in *Metaphysics* Lambda 6 by insisting that there must be some eternal substance that is immobile.[41] His justification for this claim is that substances are "the firsts of all things" (πρῶται τῶν ὄντων), and if these are all corruptible, then everything will be corruptible. Since this justification clearly presupposes a relationship of dependence between substance and other things, I think that the relevant criterion of priority can be supplied from the end of the previous chapter (i.e. Lambda 5). This would mean that eternal and unchanging substance is prior by nature to sensible and corruptible substance.In spite of its paradoxical appearance (since "nature" is defined as a principle of motion *in* things), such a result is consistent with his argument in the *Physics* for the existence of a Prime Mover from the fact of eternal motion; cf. 258b10ff. At the metaphysical level, the natural priority of the Prime Mover means that it is the paradigm case of substance. But, since 'being' is a πρὸς ἕν equivocal, the principles of the paradigm case should be applicable to all other things insofar as they are beings. Perhaps this is what Aristotle has in mind when he says that the causes of substances are the causes of all things. This is easy enough to understand if we take the primary instance of substance to be an individual living thing, since its four causes can be applied analogically to entities falling under the other categories. But it is much more difficult to see how this can be the case if we take the Prime Mover as the paradigm instance of being. It does not have either a material or a moving cause, for instance, and hence is atypical with respect to our ordinary experience of substance in the sensible world. Furthermore, it is not usual for corruptible things to have formal and final causes that are identical in every respect and at all times. Still, in spite of these difficulties, I think that Aristotle does consider the Prime Mover to be definitive for the concept of being and this is the key to understanding his description of first philosophy as "theology."[42] At any rate, it is not part of my task here to resolve this age-old problem in Aristotelian scholarship but rather to show the importance of becoming clear about senses of priority before attempting to resolve it.[43]

The concept of priority that Aristotle uses in connection with the Prime Mover is a very rich one in that it encompasses a number of the senses that have been outlined in this monograph. Naturally, the Prime Mover is prior in substance, even if one appeals to the criterion of priority inherited from the Platonists. In fact, Aristotle thinks that all other things in the universe are dependent on it as the ultimate source of motion, whereas it exists by itself independent of anything else; cf. 1072a25ff. Some previous thinkers, such as Leucippus and Plato, are acknowledged as having come close to this conception when they posited an eternal actuality (ἀεὶ ἐνέργειαν) as a constant source of motion; cf. Met. 1071b32ff. But they are criticized for not saying why or what this motion is or why it moves things in this way rather than that. Clearly, Aristotle thinks that none of his predecessors have grasped the essential nature of the Prime Mover in such a way as to answer these questions. For instance, he reports that Plato posits "that which moves itself" (τὸ αὐτὸ ἑαυτὸ κινοῦν) as a principle, yet he makes the soul contemporaneous with the universe (ἅμα τῷ οὐρανῷ) and therefore posterior (ὕστερον); cf. Met. 1071b37–1072a3. In order to convict him of treating the soul as both prior and posterior, Aristotle seems to be drawing here on Plato's dialogues.[44] Within the context of Metaphysics Lambda 6, however, it is clear that priority in actuality is the predominant meaning in question. This is the crucial sense in which the Prime Mover is prior and it encompasses priority in substance because an eternal substance is complete actuality; cf. Met. 1071b19ff. Given the description of the contemplative activity of the Prime Mover in Lambda 7, I think it is safe to conclude that Aristotle would also consider it to be prior in the sense of the best and the most honorable; cf. Met. 1072a34–b1. Indeed, it is rather appropriate that the strangest sense of priority (according to the Categories) should be recovered from ordinary language and applied to the divine.

Priority in Motion

With reference to the Prime Mover, I think we should make a digression into the *Physics* so as to explore how Aristotle uses another sense of priority in his argument for the necessary action of such a being in the universe. Even though the argument is mainly physical in character, it obviously has deep metaphysical implications, some of which we have already examined.[45] I shall make no attempt to rehearse the whole argument of Book 8, however, but will concentrate instead on chapter 7, which has a direct bearing on my chosen topic. The previous chapter has established that the permanence of motion in the universe requires the existence of some eternal and immovable mover that causes a single and simple motion; cf. *Phy.* 260a15–19. This suggests a new line of inquiry, which is taken up in the subsequent chapter and which Aristotle formulates in the following questions: (i) whether or not there can be a continuous motion, and if so, (ii) what that motion is, and (iii) which of the motions is primary (τίς πρώτη τῶν κινήσεων); cf. *Phy.* 260a21–23. The connection between the final question and the previous two is not immediately obvious, but Aristotle explains it in the following passage:

> For it is clear that if indeed a motion must always exist and if some one motion is primary and continuous, then it is this motion that the first mover causes, and this motion must be one and the same as well as continuous and primary.[46]

Here he lays out the rationale for the subsequent inquiry in terms of the cosmological role of the Prime Mover as the origin of eternal motion in the universe. Since he has proved in chapter 1 that motion must be eternal[47] and he will show that some one motion is primary and continuous, it is obvious to Aristotle that this motion will be caused by the unmoved mover and that it will be unique and simple. Thus we can see the great cosmological significance of establishing what this motion is and of proving that it is prior to all other kinds of motion.

Aristotle begins the inquiry in characteristic fashion by giving us a preview of his conclusion; i.e. that among the three kinds of motion (τριῶν . . . κινήσεων) locomotion is prior to changes with respect to magnitude and affection. In order to support this claim he then proceeds to give a number of arguments that I will merely summarize here to show how some of them are based upon priority. The first argument establishes an internal ordering among kinds of motion as follows: locomotion, alteration, increase/decrease. There Aristotle appeals to the physical thesis that growth presupposes alteration because the growing thing is increased either by what is like

or unlike and both processes involve alteration; cf. *Phy.* 260a29ff. But alteration, in turn, requires locomotion because the mover changes in place
with reference to the thing altered. Thus locomotion is prior to all other
kinds of motion because they could not exist without it.[48]

A second argument seems to depend on the old thesis of the natural philosophers[49] that the principle of all affections is condensation or rarefaction
because heaviness and lightness, hardness and softness, hotness and cold-
ness are all thought to be kinds of density or rarity; cf. *Phy.* 260b7ff. Even
the generation or corruption of substances is said to be due to the changes
in place that are responsible for condensation or rarefaction. Thus, according to this physical way of thinking, locomotion is prior to generation and
corruption. While this is a rather surprising result, it is not merely one of
the *doxa* of the natural philosophers because Aristotle defends this view
later with another argument from priority; cf. 260b26–29.

After giving two arguments for the priority of locomotion that one might
characterize as "physical," Aristotle begins a new set of arguments from a
different perspective that could plausibly be described as "logical"; cf. *Phy.*
260b15ff. While there is sufficient evidence elsewhere[50] for such a distinction in his thought, what clinches the matter here is the way he introduces
the arguments with a preliminary outline of the different senses of priority
as follows:

> Now as in other things, so also in motions the term "primary" is used in many
> senses. A thing is said to be prior to other things (a) if the others cannot exist
> without its existence but it can exist without theirs, (b) if it is prior in time to
> them, (c) if it is prior to them with respect to substance.[51]

From our previous discussions, we can immediately identify (a) as a formulation of the criterion of nonreciprocal dependence that was said to
have been used by Plato for priority with respect to nature and substance.
Since we saw this to be based upon logical relations of dependence, let us
say that it determines priority in being, so as to avoid confusion with
Aristotle's own sense of priority in substance that is also listed as (c). This
distinction is confirmed by the sort of argument he develops around each
sense of priority.

The first argument appeals to some value notions that we might identify
as part of Aristotle's Platonic heritage; e.g. that we must assume a tendency
toward perfection in nature wherever possible.[52] The argument itself assumes as established that there must exist continuous motion and proceeds
to distinguish two modes of such motion; i.e. continuous and successive.
But (the argument goes on) continuous motion has a higher degree of being

(μᾶλλον) and is better (βέλτιον) than successive motion. Since this is simply asserted as a self-evident proposition, I think we may suspect Aristotle to be falling back on an Academic assumption. This seems to be confirmed when he states another assumption of the argument that looks Academic in origin: "we always assume that the better belongs in nature, if this is possible."[53] A noteworthy aspect of this whole argument is how carefully Aristotle identifies his basic assumptions and distinguishes them from postulates that are proved elsewhere. For instance, he indicates clearly he is assuming for the moment that continuous motion is possible but that this will later be proved; cf. *Phy.* 260b23–24. Furthermore, since this motion can be identified with locomotion, the latter must be the primary motion (ἀνάγκη τὴν φορὰν εἶναι πρώτην). As if to verify this conclusion, he applies a criterion of priority as follows:

> For there is no necessity for an object in locomotion to be increasing (or decreasing) or to be in the process of generation or destruction, but none of these (changes) can exist if there is no continuous motion, which is caused by the primary mover.[54]

Here we have a concrete application of the criterion of nonreciprocal dependence,[55] which is used by way of explanation for the priority in being of continuous locomotion. Whereas it is not necessary for a locomotive (τὸ φερόμενον) either to be growing or to be altered (οὔτε αὔξεσθαι οὔτε ἀλλοιοῦσθαι) or to be generated or destroyed (οὐδε ... γίγνεσθαι ἢ φθείρεσθαι), none of these kinds of motion can 'exist' without the continuous locomotion which is caused by the primary mover. If we read the final phrase of the passage as a reference to the Prime Mover, I think we must take it as a conclusion which depends on the explicit assumption made earlier that the primary mover will cause the primary kind of motion; i.e. locomotion.

There is a second sense in which locomotion is prior to other kinds of motion; namely, prior in time. Here Aristotle begins with the explanatory remark that this is the only kind of motion possible in eternal things; cf. *Phy.* 260b29–30. Now, one might well be puzzled by this explanation because eternal things are outside time rather than temporally prior to corruptible things. But I think it is possible to make sense of Aristotle's remark within the cosmological framework that he shares with Plato. We recall that in the *Timaeus* the circular locomotion of the heavenly bodies is the embodiment of time that itself is characterized as "the moving image of eternity" (εἰκὼ ... κινητόν ... αἰῶνος); cf. 37D. Since that circular motion is itself what is numbered to yield time, there is a clear sense in which it is prior in time to other kinds of motion. Even though Aristotle disagrees with Plato about the generation of time, he follows much the same conceptual line in characterizing it as "the number of motion with respect to a prior and a posterior."[56] Similarly, he accepts that cosmic time is found by numbering the motion of the heavenly bodies, which is none other than locomotion. Therefore it makes sense for him to explain the temporal priority of locomotion by referring to the claim that this is the only kind of motion eternal things can have, though the principal meaning of such priority is found with reference to generated things.[57]

In the case of a particular generated thing, however, it would seem that locomotion is not prior but rather posterior in time. In fact, Aristotle insists that in such cases locomotion must be the latest (ὑστάτην) of all kinds of motion because it belongs to things already completed; cf. *Phy.* 260b32–33. He must be thinking of a biological example when he says that, after the generation, there will first be alteration and growth before there is locomotion. From such examples it would appear that generation is prior in time to locomotion, since the thing must be generated before it can move from place to place. Aristotle accepts that this is true for any single individual among generated things but insists upon a broader perspective; cf. *Phy.* 261a1ff. He argues that, prior to any generated individual, there must be another individual in motion but not in the process of being generated. In simple biological terms, this is the claim that the generation of any individual is preceded by the locomotion of a mature adult of the same species, while the same is true, in turn, for the generation of that individual. Thus Aristotle thinks that generation cannot be the primary kind of motion, otherwise all moved things would be destructible.[58] The implicit assumption of this brief argument is that whatever motion is primary must belong universally to all moved things.[59] But locomotion is the only motion that can belong to eternal things like the heavenly bodies that are in motion. Hence this argument gives us a straightforward way of understanding the initial remark in Aristotle's discussion of the priority in time of locomotion.[60]

Furthermore, he seems to draw upon some internal hierarchy among kinds of motions in his additional argument to the effect that none of the "succeeding motions" (τῶν ἐφεξῆς κινήσεως) are prior in time to locomotion; cf. *Phy.* 261a7ff. He hastens to explain that he is referring to growth and alteration and decrease and destruction because all of these are posterior (ὕστεραι) to generation. But, since generation cannot be prior to locomotion (for the reasons given above), neither can any of the other kinds of changes. Thus, even though an exception must be made on the individual level, it is generally true that locomotion is prior in time to all other species of change. On the cosmological level, the deeper implication of this result is that the Prime Mover is the direct cause of locomotion and not of generation or of any other kind of change in the universe.

Finally, Aristotle constructs an argument for locomotion being prior with respect to substance (κατ' οὐσίαν) by appealing to a teleological principle that might even be accepted by the Platonists. In general, he says, the thing being generated seems to be incomplete (ἀτελὲς) and "on its way to a principle" (ἐπ' ἀρχὴν ἰόν), so that what is posterior in generation is prior by nature.[61] Such a teleological principle is most plausible when applied to the biological development of an individual toward full maturity. This final stage may be seen as the principle guiding the previous stages that are incomplete with reference to it. While Aristotle is obviously appealing to his own notion of a final cause, he may be trading upon its identity with the formal cause in biological beings so as to enlist the agreement of the Platonists. Indeed, when he talks about the generated thing being on its way to a principle, he may be echoing the distinction he attributes to Plato elsewhere between the ways to and from a principle; cf. *EN* 1095a30ff. Be that as it may, the teleological principle enables Aristotle to make a sharp contrast between the temporal order of generation and the substantial order of nature. Thus it is upon such a principle that he constructs his argument for the priority of locomotion with respect to substance.

He begins by stressing that, among all the changes that belong to things in generation, locomotion is the final one (τελευταῖον); cf. *Phy.* 261a14ff. Therefore, he argues, plants and some species of animal are immobile because of some deficiency (δι' ἔνδειαν) with respect to organs, whereas locomotion belongs to species that are completed (τελειουμένοις). This constant repetition of variations upon the basic notion of *telos* indicates an argumentative strategy that depends upon the assumption that there is an internal hierarchy in nature itself. This assumption is partially formulated in the *protasis* of the subsequent conditional argument as follows: "If locomotion belongs to a higher degree to those living things which have received a nature to a greater extent. . ."[62] Here we have two implicit hierarchies that run parallel to each other: it is assumed that things can partake more or less in locomotion depending on whether they receive a higher or lower nature. This assumption is taken to ground the conclusion of the argument as expressed in the *apodosis:* "this kind of motion would be prior to the others with respect to substance."[63] The close link between the nature or substance of a thing and its characteristic locomotion is strengthened further by the consideration that a thing in locomotion departs least of all from its substance; cf. *Phy.* 261a20–21. Alone among the kinds of motion, locomotion does not involve a change of being (τοῦ εἶναι) in the thing, whereas changes in quality or quantity do. But the clearest indication of this priority for Aristotle is that locomotion is the characteristic and special motion caused by 'what moves itself.'[64] Therefore (he reports) "we say" (φαμὲν) that the self-mover is the principle (ἀρχὴν) both of things in motion and of movers, while it is also first (πρῶτον) among things in motion; cf. *Phy.* 261a25–26. In this passage it is hard to ignore the repeated use of words emphasizing the priority of the self-mover and of its typical motion, i.e. locomotion. What may be less obvious is that Aristotle tries to enlist the agreement of the Platonists by appealing to commonly accepted descriptions of the self-mover as the first principle of all motion.[65] This makes for a convincing dialectical argument that locomotion is prior to all other motions with respect to substance, since it is the principal and characteristic motion of self-movers. So it is plausible to assume that the peculiar locomotion of living things is a direct expression of their substantial form.

As a result of all these arguments, Aristotle takes it that he has adequately shown the priority of locomotion in all the relevant senses. From the amount of space devoted to this conclusion, we can guess that it is an important step in the whole argument of *Physics* VIII for the necessity of the Prime Mover as the source of motion in the universe.[66] Since the nature of the Prime Mover dictates that it cause only one simple motion, it is crucial for Aristotle's argument that this motion be prior in every sense to all other motions on the cosmic level, otherwise his universe may disintegrate into a series of episodes like a bad tragedy; cf. *Met.* XII, 10, 1076a1–4. Having established the complete priority of locomotion, the subsequent step of his inquiry is to identify the kind of locomotion that can be both continuous and eternal. On account of the unique and simple action of the Prime Mover, it must cause motion that satisfies these two conditions. I do not propose to pursue any further the details of this argument, since my chosen task was to show how the different senses of priority play an important role in Aristotle's theory about the action of the Prime Mover in his universe.[67]

Priority and Mathematical Objects

Finally let me turn to *Metaphysics* Mu 2 where Aristotle distinguishes between different senses of priority in order to answer those Platonists who posit mathematical objects as independent substances separate from and prior to sensible things. Appropriately enough, this will bring us back full circle to our initial discussion of the passage in the *Topics,* where there is some ambiguity about Aristotle's position on the ontological status of mathematical objects. In Mu 2, however, there is no ambiguity about his efforts to refute Platonism through many dialectical arguments. Even though it is impossible for me to consider these arguments in detail, I want to distinguish generally between two strategies that he adopts in his attempted refutations. First, through shared assumptions, he teases out *internal* contradictions within the views of different Platonists about the mode of being of mathematical objects. Second, he emphasizes the way such views conflict *externally* with commonsense assumptions about the nature of reality.

It is this second prong of attack that is most revealing for my purposes here, since it makes extensive use of the notion of priority. For instance, it begins with an argument that appeals directly to truth and to accepted beliefs about substance. The argument goes as follows:

> In general, if one posits the mathematical objects as natures which are separate, conclusions contrary both to truth and to the accepted beliefs will follow. For these natures, because they are posited as such, must be prior to sensible magnitudes, but with respect to truth they must be posterior; for the incomplete magnitude is prior in generation but posterior in substance to the completed magnitude. For example, this is how the lifeless is related to the living.[68]

The emphatic position of the word ὅλως in the Greek signals a move to a more general critique of the mathematical ontology of the Platonists. The view being criticized is set out as the *protasis* of a conditional as follows: "If one posits mathematical objects to be in this way as some separated natures. . ."[69] The difficulties for such a view, which here constitute Aristotle's objection, are described generally in the *apodosis* as consequences that conflict with truth and the usual assumptions.[70] For instance, as Aristotle explains, one consequence will be that mathematical objects, on account of having such a mode of being (διὰ τὸ μὲν οὕτως εἶναι), must be prior to sensible magnitudes (προτέρας εἶναι τῶν αἰσθητῶν μεγεθῶν). This consequence is contrary to truth because, in fact, they are posterior (ὑστέρας) to such magnitudes. Since we have not previously come across this sense of priority with respect to truth (κατὰ τὸ ἀληθὲς), we might wonder about its exact meaning here.[71] But I think that we can safely assume it to be another way of expressing the kind of priority with respect to actuality (κατ' ἐντελέχειαν) that we found to be explicated at Delta 11 and Theta 8.

My assumption seems to be confirmed by Aristotle's subsequent explanation in terms of the distinction between what is prior in generation (γενέσει) and what is prior in substance (τῇ οὐσίᾳ). Obviously he is referring to mathematical objects when he concedes that "incomplete magnitude" (ἀτελὲς μέγεθος) may be prior with respect to generation but insists that it is posterior with respect to substance. Thus it is plausible to assume that posteriority in substance corresponds to posteriority with respect to truth, which was mentioned in the previous line. In order to preserve the contrast being made in that line, however, one must also assume that priority with respect to substance is held to be a consequence of the separation of mathematical objects. Furthermore, this would be consistent with an application of the criterion of priority with respect to nature and substance that is attributed to Plato at Delta 11. According to this criterion, mathematical magnitudes would be prior in substance to sensible magnitudes if they could exist independently of them, while the reverse was not the case. It is quite likely that Aristotle is appealing to some such criterion here when from the Platonist position he draws conclusions that are described as contrary to truth. When he talks about "incomplete magnitude," however, it does appear as if he were introducing a different criterion of priority so as to reach his own conclusions. Yet I think that we should not be too quick to accuse Aristotle of cheating, since such a move was part and parcel of his dialectical strategy in refuting opponents.[72]

It is clear, for instance, that he introduces some criterion of completeness in order to distinguish between priority in generation and priority in substance,[73] which were presumably identified by the Platonists. According to their principles, as we have seen, the order of 'generation' of magnitudes from point to line to plane to solid corresponds exactly to their ordering with respect to substance. But these orders are completely reversed when the notion of completeness is applied to the schema because now the solid appears to be most complete. If what is complete is also more independent, then we have a reversal of priority in substance even when we apply the distinctively Platonic criterion.

I think that the crucial move in Aristotle's strategy here is to show that the independence of things must be defined in terms of their completeness. This is what I see him trying to do in a later passage at Mu 2 that describes the 'generation' of magnitudes in the following terms:

> Again, the way generation proceeds may clarify the matter. For what is generated first is something with length, then with width, lastly with depth, and the completion has been attained. Accordingly, if that which is posterior in generation is prior in substance, the body would be prior to the plane and the line, and as such it would be complete and whole to a higher degree than they are, seeing that it can also become animate. But how can a line or a plane be animate? Such an axiom is beyond our senses.[74]

If this passage is to give a dialectical refutation of his opponents, it must have been the case that they spoke about the 'generation' of magnitudes in three stages, ending with the third dimension.[75] Even if they did, however, there was an established tradition within the Academy that such terms were to be used only in a metaphorical sense for the sake of teaching and learn-ing.[76] But Aristotle typically seizes upon such talk in order to show that his opponents implicitly acknowledge some kind of goal to the process of 'gen-eration.' This is obvious, for instance, in the way that he describes the final stage of generation, i.e. depth, as having reached its goal.[77]

Having seized on this shared teleological perspective, Aristotle now ap-plies the metaphysical principle that governs his own teleological thinking; i.e. what is posterior in generation is prior in substance.[78] Of course, this is none other than the criterion of priority with respect to actuality that we found elaborated in Theta 8. According to this criterion, therefore, the body (τὸ σῶμα) would be prior to the plane and the line. In addition, Aristotle thinks that the body is complete (τέλειον) and more of a whole (ὅλον μᾶλλον) precisely because it can become animate (ὅτι ἔμψυχον γίγνεται). This means that he has subtly introduced a biological (and hence physical) criterion for the priority in substance of bodies over lines and planes. This is confirmed by the subsequent rhetorical question, How could a line or a plane be animate? Obviously his point is that when something is alive we actually perceive it to have some kind of motion and this is not the case for planes or lines. But since it is highly unlikely that any of the Platonists held planes or lines to be alive, Aristotle may be simply making this argument for rhetorical effect so as to convince his listeners of the ab-surdity of positing mathematical objects as independent substances.[79]

The argument is made plausible by the introduction of completeness as a requirement for substantial independence because completeness, in turn, can be judged by sense perception in terms of the capacity of something for becoming animate. Furthermore, according to Aristotle's account, the cri-terion of completeness was implicitly accepted by the Platonists them-selves when they talked about the 'generation' of mathematical magni-tudes. Thus their claim that lines and planes are separate substances tends to be undermined by the logic of their own language. This is the sort of dialectical reversal that is very dear to Aristotle's heart, and in order to produce it, he may be distorting the Platonic account. But it is not part of my task here to judge the fairness or otherwise of his dialectical practice.[80]

To conclude this section, let me examine a passage from the end of Mu 2 where I think that Aristotle makes a small concession to the Platonists while simultaneously revising a position he seems to have held in the *Top-ics*. Immediately prior to this passage, he has argued that planes or lines or points cannot even be substantial in the material sense in which a body is a kind of substance (οὐσία τις ὑλική), since nothing appears to be capable of being composed from them. But, he continues:

Let it be granted that they are prior in formula to the body. But it is not always the case that what is prior in formula is also prior in substance. For A is prior in substance to B if A surpasses B in existing separately, but A is prior in formula to B if the formula of A is a part of the formula of B; and the two priorities do not belong to the same thing together. For if attributes, as for example a motion of some kind or whiteness, do not exist apart from substances, whiteness is prior in formula to the white man but not prior in substance; for whiteness cannot exist separately but exists always in the composite. So, it is evident that neither is the thing abstracted prior, nor is what results by addition posterior; for it is by addition of whiteness that we speak of a white man.[81]

The prominence of the concessive μὲν in this passage indicates Aristotle's willingness to concede that mathematical objects are prior in formula (τῷ ... λόγῳ ... πρότερα) to bodies (as implied by the context). But he immediately minimizes the concession by countering that not all things that are prior in formula are also prior in substance.[82] In order to underline this distinction, he offers different criteria for the two kinds of priority. Since these criteria are rather convoluted and formulaic, let us adopt Apostle's convention of lettering for the purpose of explanation. Thus, the criterion of substantial priority would go as follows: A is prior in substance to B if A surpasses B in 'existing' separately (ὅσα χωριζόμενα τῷ εἶναι ὑπερβάλλει).[83] By comparison, the criterion of priority in formula would be: A is prior in formula to B if the formula of A is part of the formula of B (ὅσων οἱ λόγοι ἐκ τῶν λόγων). As if for emphasis, Aristotle insists that two types of priority do not belong simultaneously to the same thing (ταῦτα δὲ οὐχ ἅμα ὑπάρχει). In the light of our previous discussions of such priorities, however, I think we must take him to mean that the two types of priority do not *usually* belong together to the same things.

In support of this interpretation, we could point to *Metaphysics* Zeta 1, where Aristotle implies that priority in definition (λόγῳ) and priority in substance coincide in the same thing when it is a primary substance; cf. *Met.*1028a31–33. But we should recall that the explanation of priority in definition given there is quite different from the criterion listed here at Mu 2, and this should make us suspect that a special sense of λόγος is being introduced to deal with the case of mathematical objects.[84] Translators and commentators who render this as "formula" have the right instinct, I think, since it can hardly mean "definition" in the strict sense of an account of the essence; cf. Zeta 4 and 5.[85] In fact, the examples used to illustrate this kind of priority indicate that Aristotle has in mind instances where an accidental attribute must be defined before the whole of which it is a nonessential part. For instance, 'the white' is prior to 'the white man' in this rather innocuous sense. If we wish to nail down this special sense of priority, we can simply return to the passage in Delta 11, where Aristotle says that the accident is prior to the whole with respect to account.[86] The parallel is clinched when he gives the example of 'the musical' being prior to 'the musical man.' By way of explanation for this kind of priority, he falls back on the truism that the whole account cannot *be* without the part. Such an explanation becomes more relevant to the present passage in Mu 2 when Aristotle enters the caveat that 'the musical' cannot 'exist' without some being that is musical.[87] We can compare this with the warning given here against thinking the priority in formula of whiteness implies that it is somehow independent of white things. For instance, he says that it cannot 'exist' separately but is always along with the composite.[88] It is clear from the immediate context that this dependent mode of being attributed to whiteness is directly connected with the denial that it is prior in substance to white things.

Confirmation of such a connection can be found in the implicit appeal to his own categories that is contained in the *protasis* of the following conditional statement: "If attributes do not exist apart from substances (εἰ . . . μὴ ἔστι τὰ πάθη παρὰ τὰς οὐσίας) then 'the white' may be prior to 'the white man' with respect to formula but not with respect to substance (ἀλλ' οὐ κατὰ τὴν οὐσίαν)." In other words, the dependent ontological status of an attribute like whiteness has definite implications for the sort of priority that may be given to it. Even though an example from the category of quantity is not given, one must presume that Aristotle intends the same to hold for mathematical objects. Thus he concludes that the object resulting from abstraction is not prior nor is the object resulting from addition posterior.[89] While he concedes to the Platonists that such abstract objects may be prior in formula, he insists that they are not independent substances. Of course, he does not deny that mathematical objects have some mode of being, since 'being' has many senses; cf. *Met.* 1077b17. But with respect to this passage in Mu 2, I think it is just as important to be clear about the many senses of 'priority' in order to define his opposition to the Platonists.[90]

This point can be made clearer by recalling once more the passage in Delta 11 that attributed to Plato the sense of priority with respect to nature and substance. In connection with that passage I have already argued that the criterion of dependence used there can be made to yield the result that point, line, and plane are more substantial than body, if we make the Platonic assumption that the order of being follows the order of knowledge. I think it is clear that a crucial part of Aristotle's break with Platonism in mathematics involves a revision of this assumption. At the end of Mu 2, for instance, when he admits that mathematical objects may be prior in formula to body yet denies that they are more substantial than it, he is revising an assumption that he appears to have accepted in the *Topics;* namely, that the greater intelligibility of points, lines, and planes gives them priority by nature over bodies. Now that sense perception is made the touchstone of substantiality,[91] we might even conjecture that Aristotle has returned to that "ordinary understanding" (τῆς τυχούσης ... διανοίας) of which he spoke in the earlier work; cf. *Top.* 141b13–14. In contrast to the accurate (ἀκριβοῦς) and "odd" (περιττῆς) understanding of mathematicians, most people grasp the solid before the plane because it is more obvious to perception. Thus, if one frames definitions according to the order of perception, the plane might be defined as the limit of the solid; cf. *Top.* 141b19–23. Whereas in the *Topics* such a definition was implied to be less scientific because it cannot show the essence of the definiendum, it is not clear whether Aristotle would still hold this in the *Metaphysics*. Even on his own mature view of essential definition, it must be the case that the mode of being an entity (and especially the subject to which it belongs *per se*) is somehow reflected in this definition. Thus he would probably be inclined to say that the definition of a plane as the limit of a solid is more appropriate *ontologically,* while the Academic definition in terms of surrounding lines is a better *logical* definition. It was precisely the absence of such a distinction in the *Topics* that made his metaphysical stance rather ambiguous but there is little doubt about his anti-Platonism in *Metaphysics* Mu.

Conclusion

What I have attempted to do in this chapter is to achieve a new perspective on some of Aristotle's characteristic metaphysical positions by showing how distinctions between the prior and the posterior underlie them in different ways. At the beginning of *Metaphysics* Zeta, for instance, he claims that substance is prior in every sense and then proceeds to delineate his own conception of substance in opposition to the Platonists and other predecessors. I have tried to show how the preeminence of biological form as substance is established through the use of criteria that presuppose 'being' and, consequently, 'priority' to have the logical structure of *pros hen* equivocals. Thus equipped, Aristotle rejects the claims of Platonic dialectic to be the mistress science of reality, since he argues that Forms or universals are not the focal referents of 'being.' Similarly, in Epsilon, he makes the existence of First Philosophy (as distinct from physics) depend upon whether there is an immobile substance apart from and prior to sensible substance. Digressing into the *Physics,* we find that the existence of the Prime Mover is closely related to the argument for the absolute priority of circular locomotion in the universe. In *Metaphysics* Mu, by contrast, Aristotle denies that mathematical objects are separated substances, while conceding that they may be prior to sensible things in a purely logical sense. We should recall once more that this represents a reversal of a Platonic schema of priority with respect to substance, which Aristotle seems to have accepted without demur in parts of the *Topics*.

Conclusion

IN THIS STUDY I HAVE TRIED TO ESTABLISH A FRESH PERSPECTIVE FROM WHICH TO understand better the development of Aristotle's metaphysical thinking, with special reference to the many senses of priority. By taking the question about the ontological status of mathematical objects as my point of departure, I have shown the central role that the concept of priority plays in his thinking about substance. As certain passages in the *Topics* and *Categories* show, he seems to have initially accepted a Platonic schema of natural priority, which implies that genera are more substantial than species and which gives greater reality to mathematical entities than to sensible bodies. Against such an Academic background, we can see that Aristotle's logical and metaphysical thinking is heavily influenced by the Socratic "turn to the *logoi*" that determined the direction of the whole Platonic tradition. Since Aristotelian philosophy is firmly embedded in that tradition, it should not really surprise us that Aristotle begins by accepting the ontological primacy of entities that are the paradigmatic objects of mathematics and dialectic.

Furthermore, given the Academic preoccupation with language as a guide to how things are, it is quite understandable that Aristotle should collect the many senses of priority in the *Categories* while giving pride of place to a Platonic schema of priorities. Later, however, he establishes an alternative schema of priorities that conforms better to his own metaphysical orientation and we find this delineated in *Metaphysics* Delta 11, together with the meanings of priority that are embedded in language and are inherited from previous philosophical traditions. In fact, this chapter from Aristotle's philosophical dictionary encapsulates in many ways the development of his thinking about priority and its relationship to substance. In view of his continued use of Academic criteria of priority, perhaps it is an exaggeration to talk about Aristotle's "break" with Platonism, though we should notice a definite move away from mathematical and dialectical conceptions of substance.

But his mature position on substance and priority is spelled out more clearly in the central books of the *Metaphysics,* where substance as biological form is held to be prior in all the important senses. Even when Aristotle concedes to the Platonists that mathematical objects are prior in a certain way, it turns out to be an unimportant sense of priority. This provides us with clear evidence that he considered the notion of priority to be crucial for the elucidation of his metaphysical position vis-à-vis his philosophical predecessors. In opposition to the natural philosophers whom he saw as giving primacy to matter, Aristotle emphasized the primacy of form; while he differentiates himself from the other philosophers of form by insisting upon the characteristic teleology of biological form as against that of mathematical form. Furthermore, he replaces the notion of a "mistress science" of dialectic with a departmentalization of the sciences, which presumably reflects his view that being is not univocal but is rather said in many senses. Yet 'being' (like 'priority') is not simply equivocal and so Aristotle envisages the possibility of developing a single science of reality that studies substance as the primary instance of being and, thereby, studies the whole of being.

Thus, when we examine the perennial question about whether Aristotle's science of metaphysics is a theology or a general ontology, we find the concept of priority to be central to his attempt to reconcile these two opposing tendencies in his thought. Furthermore, the unity of his metaphysics seems to turn on the question of whether divine being is the primary instance of substance or of being. This question is paralleled in Aristotle's *Physics* by the cosmological question about what kind of change in the universe is directly caused by the Prime Mover. In general, we discover that the Aristotelian conceptual system is constructed upon hierarchies and schemata of priority that are motivated by some version of the Platonic 'degrees-of-being' thesis. I think this is sufficient justification for my lengthy attempt to clarify the different senses of priority in Aristotle's logical and metaphysical thought.

NOTES

BIBLIOGRAPHY

INDEX

NOTES

Introduction

1. For example, Alexander, Aquinas, Ross, Kirwan, and Apostle (to give just a cross-section) all give pride of place in their commentaries to the several senses of being. Even though Alexander also gives more attention to this point (cf. *In Metaph.* 240,31–243,28; 373,1–376, 12; 459,4–460,30 (Hayduck)), still he does not neglect the many senses of priority according to Aristotle (cf. 384,33–388,4; 460,31–461,35). In this much, at least, he is more balanced than modern commentators.

2. Since it is impossible to review all the literature, let us take Ross and Owens as representative examples. Ross (1924 i, pp. cxxviii–cxxxx, 316–18; ii, pp. 160–61) sets the precedent by giving priority very little attention. He also claims that Aristotle is careless about preserving the same appelations for the various senses of 'prior' and, in support of this claim, he cites some passages where Aristotle seems to be using priority in φύσις and οὐσία in senses that differ from those listed in *Metaphysics* V, 11; VII, 1. Through analysis of such passages, I hope to make these discrepancies intelligible from the perspective of the development of new problems. Owens (1951, pp. 319–22, 330, 406, 438) shows a certain improvement in the understanding of the role of 'priority' in Aristotle's conceptual framework when he gives an excellent summary of its different meanings (pp. 319–21). Yet, Owens (p. 330) tends to assume that the same meaning of priority should carry over throughout a particular discussion, and other remarks (p. 321) about Aristotle's failure to preserve the "systematic divisions" of priority show a certain lack of understanding on Owens' part about how the concept and its governing criteria function. An exception to the general neglect of priority in Aristotle is Philippe (1969, pp. 1–74), who explicitly acknowledges the importance of this question of what he calls "anteriority and posteriority" (p. 48) and also "previous and consequent" (p. 49). But, as I shall note in the appropriate places, his interpretation does not seem to be based on a close reading of Aristotle's text.

3. In addition, this would seem to commit Aristotle to a thesis about degrees of being, which is usually associated with Plato's metaphysical framework; cf. Vlastos 1973, pp. 43–57, 58–75. My understanding of this aspect of Aristotelian metaphysics has been enriched by conversations with Donald Morrison and by acquaintance with his work on the topic; cf. unpublished MS 1 and 1987.

4. Perhaps I should warn the reader that this monograph does not try to give a complete survey of all the occurrences and usages of 'prior' and 'posterior' in the Aristotelian corpus. While such a survey would not be without its own intrinsic interest for the specialist, I have chosen to concentrate upon the surveys given by Aristotle himself because these show us something about the development of his conception of priority and posteriority, as well as about how such concepts are applied in his logical and metaphysical works.

5. Cf. Merlan 1975, pp. 160–220.

6. Brentano 1862.

7. Reasonably complete lists of passages for the occurrence of πρότερον and ὕστερον in Platonic and Aristotelian texts can be found in Bonitz 1870, pp. 652–54, 806–7; Ast 1835, pp. 215–16, 462–63; and Brandwood 1976, pp. 798, 924.

8. In Ockham's logic, for instance, we find the distinction between *a priori* and *a posteriori* demonstration being linked with Aristotle's distinction between demonstration of the reasoned fact (propter quid) and of the fact (quia); cf. *Sum. Log.* III, 2, c. 17–19.

9. Cf. Gram 1968.

10. In reply to the question "Demandabo causam et rationem quare opium facit dormire?", Molière's 'doctus bachielierus' replied: "Quiat est in eo virtus dormitiva, cuius est natura sensus assoupire."

11. At *De Anima* II, 3, 414b23, Aristotle claims that there is no definition of the concept indicating the prior and the posterior, which seems to put it in the same logical situation as 'one' and 'being'.

12. If we consult any handbook of scholastic metaphysics, we do not find 'prior' and 'posterior' being treated under the rubric of transcendentals; cf. De Raeymaeker, 1935. Even if Aristotle dithers over the central meaning of 'priority', however, that should not make any difference to the basic logical structure of a *pros hen* equivocal. But of course, not all such equivocals were also held to be transcendentals.

13. Cf. *Opus Oxon.*, lib. 1, dist. 8, quaest. 3, nn. 18–19; IX, 597b–98b.

14. Cf. *De Natura Generis*, c.2—this is listed among the doubtful works of Aquinas; cf. Busa (ed.) 1975.

15. Cf. *Quodl.* q. 19, n.5.

16. Cf. *De Prim. Prin.* C 1.7.

17. Cf. ibid. C 1.8.

18. For the connection between 'prior' and 'posterior' and Aristotle's theory of contraries, see Anton 1957, ch. IV, sec. 3: pp. 58–61.

19. Morrison (unpublished MS 1) takes Aristotle to be denying that substance-kinds like 'man' and 'animal' have degrees, given that the name of a natural kind and the expression for its essence are interchangeable in metaphysical contexts.

20. *Metaphysics* N 1, 1088b3, seems to indicate that the categories were ordered as prior and posterior with reference to substance as a principle.

21. Cf. *Met.* I, 8, 988b28–34; XII, 6, 1071b37.

22. It is possible that Aristotle's lost work, referred to as a "Selection of the Contraries" (ἐκλογὴ τῶν ἐναντίων), elucidated the notions of the prior and the posterior as part of his theory of contraries; cf. *Met.* IV, 2, 1004a2. The Platonic background to this theory is arguably the *Parmenides* dialogue that discusses most of these 'forms of being' and reduces them to an ultimate distinction between One and Plurality; cf. 129C–D, 140E–141A, 151E–155D, 154D–155E. Perhaps this is also the appropriate background for understanding the second part of the *Categories* that is now called the Postpraedicamenta. Despite its Platonic origins, however, the topic of the prior and the posterior was considered sufficiently important within the Peripatetic tradition to justify a book by Strato of Lampsacus, the successor to Theophrastus as head of the Lyceum; cf. Wehrli (ed.) 1969; Grayeff 1974, pp. 53–54.

1. Platonic Background of the *Topics*

1. The *Topics* is usually treated as a primer for dialectical practice, where Aristotle illustrates rules by means of examples from various branches of knowledge. This has prevailed as the standard view since the nineteenth century (cf. Waitz 1846, Hambruch 1904), and recent studies have not really disputed it; cf. Evans 1977.

2. *Top.* VI, 4, 141a 26–31; translated by Pickard-Cambridge in Ross (ed.) 1928.

3. Barnes (1982, p. 33) thinks that among this list of conditions, the final one (which he takes to be a combination of priority and causation) is most directly linked to Aristotle's account of what knowledge is. An essential condition of knowledge, according to that account, is that axioms state the ultimate causes of the facts expressed by the theorems that themselves depend on the axioms.

4. Barnes 1975, p. 98.

5. It should be noted here that the Greek commentators do not seem to attach any importance to the distinction between the simple and the relative senses of priority (πρῶτον/ προτέρον) perhaps because they thought that no philosophical point depends on it; cf. Themisitus, *In An. Pst.* 6,14ff. (ed. Wallies), and Philoponus, *In An. Pst.* 28,21ff. (ed. Wallies). But, even though Aristotle does not really elucidate that distinction, I will argue that it serves

some philosophical purpose. By contrast, it is not clear that he ever adverted to the distinction between terms and propositions with references to first principles; cf. *An. Pst.* II, 19, and *Met.* I, 1.

6. *An. Pst.* I, 2, 71b33–72a5: translated by Tredennick in Goold (ed.) 1960.

7. It is possible that the respective phrases πρότερον τῇ φύσει and γνωριμώτερον ἀπλῶς were derived from some quasi-technical Academic usage but the Greek commentators do not notice this and fail to keep the epithets distinct; e.g. Alexander (*In Top.* 437,23 [ed. Wallies)) seems to use τῇ φύσει as a qualifier for γνωριμώτερον as well as for πρότερον. Once again, I am indebted to Donald Morrison for drawing my attention to this point.

8. S. Mansion (1979, pp. 161–70) lists many versions of this important epistemological move throughout the works of Aristotle: (i) from particular to universal—cf. *Top.* 156a4–7, *An.Pst.* 72a4–5, *Phy.* 189a5–7, *Met.* 1018b32–34; (ii) from sensation to intellection—cf. *An.Pst.* 72a1–3, *Phy.* 188b30–32, 189a4–5; (iii) from the obscure to the more clear—cf. *De An.* 413a11–12. But I think it is slightly misleading for her to sum them all up in terms of the difference between perception and concept, since Aristotle thinks it is possible for the intellect to grasp a cause immediately through perception, and it is also possible to have less intelligible concepts, as his reviews of predecessors continually show.

9. Cf. *Metaphysics* Zeta 13–15, especially the arguments against the priority and greater substantiality of universals; e.g. 1038b23ff.

10. In the case of propositions, the absolutely prior would probably be premises that state an immediate and essential connection between subject and predicate. In such cases the predicate is usually part of the essence of the thing and so the premise would be a definition. Thus the threat of an infinite regress is headed off by the existence of such self-caused or self-explanatory facts as are expressed by definitions; cf. Barnes 1982, p. 33.

11. Ἡμεῖς δέ φαμεν οὖτε πᾶσαν ἐπιστήμην ἀποδεικτικὴν εἶναι, ἀλλὰ τὴν τῶν ἀμέσων ἀναπόδεικτον—*An. Pst.* 72b19–20.

12. ἀρχὴν ἐπιστήμης εἶναί τινά . . . ἢ τοὺς ὅρους γνωρίζομεν—*An. Pst.* 72b24–25.

13. *Cf. An. Pst.* A33, 88b36 and B 19, 100b15.

14. Cf. *An. Pst.* 72b26–32: translation by Barnes 1975, p. 6 (his italics and parentheses)

15. Cherniss (1944, p. 63, n. 51) also finds a similarity between the Platonic and Aristotelian distinctions.

16. Wieland (1960, pp. 206–19) thinks that this distinction is frequently used for protreptic purposes; i.e. to justify the possibility of gaining knowledge; cf. *Phy.* I, 184a16ff., *Met.* II, 993b1ff., and *Protr.* Fr 6 (Ross 1955).

17. ἑκάστῳ γὰρ τῶν ὄντων ἔν ἐστι τὸ εἶναι ὅπερ ἐστίν—*Top.*141a35–36. One of the most important technical uses of the Greek word ὅπερ is with reference to expressions that show precisely what the thing in question *is* or of what *kind* it is; cf. *LSJ*, p. 1262. Thus it would appear to indicate an identity between the thing and its essence—which is exactly what Aristotle needs for the above argument.

18. *Top.* VI, 4, 141b3–14; translated by Forster in Goold (ed.) 1960.

19. In spite of a lengthy discussion of this passage, however, Evans (1977, pp. 69ff.) does not feel prompted to raise such a question, since he assumes that Aristotle's critical stance toward Plato carries into every corner of his works. As should become clear from my whole monograph, I do not think this simple assumption is adequate to deal with the evidence for residual Platonism throughout his works.

20. At *Metaphysics* N 1, 1087a31ff., we find a revealing argument for the absolute priority of the principle of all things, whatever that turns out to be.

21. Such passages in Aristotle that show Academic influences are well documented by Gaiser (1962; cf. esp. Anchang; "Testimonia Platonica") in his controversial book on Plato's unwritten doctrine. Even though he would reject the whole notion of an "unwritten doctrine" of Plato, Cherniss (1944, p. 26) would not dispute the fact that the *Topics* abounds with echoes of Platonic dialogues and Academic doctrines. In fact, he approves of listening to these echoes as harbingers for Aristotle's own doctrines. If we look carefully in the works of Aristotle, we can find considerable evidence for the influence of this Academic schema of nat-

ural priority; cf. *Met.* 1019a2–3, *E.E.* 1217b11–13, and *Pol.* 1253a21. From these passages it would appear that the stock phrase for its ruling criterion was as follows: ἀναιρουμένων τῶν πρότερων . . . ἀναιρεῖται τὰ ὕστερα. Such criteria and the schemata of priority they generate seem to have been unquestioningly accepted by Aristotle in early works like the *Protrepticus,* where he says: αἰτιά τε μᾶλλον τὰ πρότερα τῶν ὑστέρων· ἐκείνων γὰρ ἀναιρουμένων ἀναιρεῖται τὰ τὴν οὐσίαν ἐξ ἐκείνων ἔχοντα, μήκη μὲν ἀριθμῶν, ἐπίπεδα δὲ μηκῶν, στερεὰ δὲ ἐπιπέδων, στοιχείων δὲ αἱ ὀνομαζομένων συγγαβαί (Iambl. *Protr.* 6, 37.34–38. 5 Pistelli); cf. Ross (ed.) 1955, p. 32. From my point of view, what is interesting about this passage is that it occurs within the context of Aristotle's argument that the prior is always more knowable than the posterior. His use of the familiar criterion and his talk of causes indicate that natural priority is intended.

22. I think that this passage also contains an illustration of the "degrees-of-reality" thesis that Plato and his followers accepted. What is even more interesting, however, is that the *Protepticus* uncritically accepts such a thesis for substances of different kinds and even within the same kind; cf. Fr. 14 (Ross 1955).

23. τὰ μὲν ἄνευ σώματος ἐνδέχεσθαι δοκεῖ εἶναι τὸ δὲ σῶμα ἄνευ τούτων ἀδύνατον— *Met.*1002a6–7.

24. Thus, in *Categories* 5, when Aristotle insists that there is no "more or less" (μᾶλλον ἢ ἧττον) among primary substances themselves, it is plausible to read him as reacting against an Academic tendency to establish value hierarchies even among what were considered to be substances. It is noteworthy that in the *Protrepticus* immediately prior to the fragment cited above (in n. 21), Aristotle establishes a direct correspondence between what is better (τὰ βελτίω) and what is more intelligible. This valuational aspect to intelligibility is justified because science is about definite and ordered objects (τῶν γὰρ ὡρισμένων καὶ τεταγμένων ἐπιστήμη μᾶλλον ἐστιν), which also turn out to be good rather than evil objects. But I think that this interconnection between goodness, intelligibility and natural priority is no accident, since it is a characteristic link made by Plato in such dialogues as the *Republic.* Thus, in a fragment from the lost work *On the Good,* Aristotle attributes to Plato and the Pythagoreans a schema of natural priority that combines numbers and Forms as absolute firsts; cf. Alex. Aphr., *In Metaph,* 55.20ff. (Fr. 2—Ross 1955).

25. Cf. *Met.* 1017b20–21, 1002a11–12.

26. Taran (1981, App. I) thinks that Speusippus may have accepted this definition of the unit based on its similarity to the point, and he cites a passage in the *Topics* (108b26–31) as his source for one of the fragments (F 65) of that Academic thinker. Proclus (*In Eucl.* 95.21–22) ascribes to the Pythagoreans the definition of the point as a monad with position, but this is consistent with it also being an Academic definition. It is difficult to know what to make of Aristotle's statement that Plato rejected the existence of the point as "a geometrical fiction," but it clearly has something to do with the tradition about indivisible lines; cf. Nicol, (1936, pp. 120–26). Furley (1967, p. 106) seems to think that Plato denied reality to the point because the indivisible line is the unit of linear measurement. Thus Furley concludes that the point has no claim to be an ἀρχή, since it is "destroyed along with" (συναναιρεῖν) the line and so is not prior to it. Yet he concedes (1967, p. 110, n. 3) that this explanation is conjectural because he acknowledges that the Academy (and probably Plato himself) later rehabilitated the point. But this concession appears to indicate a certain confusion on his part about how the criteria of priority were applied within the Academy, especially the assumption that the criteria were used to decide questions of 'existence.'

27. Cf. *Timaeus* 27D and *Republic* 477A.

28. *Top.* VI, 4, 141b15–29: my translation is loosely based on that of Forster in Goold (ed.) 1960.

29. The residue of such a tradition seems to be contained in some of the definitions that Euclid lists in his *Elements* (cf. Bk. I, defs. 3 and 6). This might be taken to indicate that the tradition was Pythagorean in origin, but I have grave doubts about this. In the above *Topics* passage, Aristotle introduces these alternative definitions as if they were typical of non-mathematical thinkers. Secondly, the ironic way in which Socrates puts forward such a defi-

nition in the *Meno* suggests that it would be more familiar to Meno than a proper scientific definition. Thus we must look to Meno's nonmathematical education by the Sophist Gorgias as a possible source for what I have called "concrete" definitions. While the influences upon Gorgias are obscure to us, we do know that generally the Sophists took a great deal from the physical philosophers; cf. the account of color in the *Meno* that is explicitly attributed to Empedocles. Now we might also point in the direction of Democritus of Abdera, who is reputed to have written some works on quasi-mathematical topics such as: "On the contact of the Circle and the Sphere" (περὶ φαύσιος κύκλου καὶ σφαίρης), which may have contained responses to the objections of Protagoras against geometers; cf. Boyer 1968, pp. 87–89, and Heath 1921, pp. 176–81.

30. πάντες γὰρ διὰ τὼν ὑστέρων τὰ πρότερα δηλοῦσιν—*Top.* 141b21.

31. Evans (1977, p. 70) thinks that the distinction between the two forms of intelligibility must be an Aristotelian discovery, even though he finds parallels with Plato's distinction between the way to and from the first principles. He makes the plausible conjecture (if we overlook his anachronistic labels) that Aristotle is trying to resolve a contemporary dispute between extreme "realists" and "relativists" about the relationship between intelligibility and definition. At one extreme there are those who insist that the definiendum is a single essence that demands a unique definition, and hence they deny that there are other accounts that may instruct us about the nature of the subject. In contrast, there are those at the other extreme who accept any such account as a definition without regard to its degree of intelligibility. By appealing to the distinction between the unqualified and qualified meanings of 'more intelligible,' Aristotle can hold on to the instructive function of definition without conceding its objective character. Thus the real definition is given in terms that are more intelligible in the absolute sense that they are instructive for the man of sound mental disposition, whereas improper definitions may be intelligible and instructive for particular persons or groups. The only quibble I have with the whole analysis given by Evans is that he fails to notice the ontological significance of the mathematical examples given to illustrate the difference between proper and improper definitions.

32. A number of scholars have recognized that this was originally a Platonist principle that later became formalized as a typical mode of argumentation; i.e. *modus a tollendo tollens;* cf. *Top.* 119a34–37, 123a14–15; *Met.* 1059b30–31, 1060a1. For discussions consult Moraux 1973, p. 156 and Wilpert 1949, p. 148.

33. τὸ γένος δοκεῖ τὴν τοῦ ὁριζομένου οὐσίαν σημαίνειν—*Top.* 139a30–31.

34. Of course, it is not easy to establish exactly what were Plato's ontological commitments. Yet I think it is arguable that in later dialogues like the *Sophist* he is committed to some kind of hierarchy among the Forms as part of his theory about their "mingling"; e.g. the theory of the "greatest kinds."

35. Cf. *Metaphysics* Zeta 13 (1038b1–1039a23) where Aristotle gives his most detailed treatment of the reasons why the universal cannot be substance. It is noteworthy that in this chapter he constructs his argument in terms of priority: It is impossible that what is a substance and a 'this,' if composed of parts, should be from a quality (i.e. a universal) because then it would be prior to substance. But (he continues) the attributes of a substance cannot be prior to it either in formula, in time, or in generation because that would imply that they are separated (χωριστά). It is clear that the argument is aimed at universals as attributes, since he later describes the common predicate, which is a universal, as a 'such' (τοιόνδε) rather than a 'this' (τόδε τι); cf. 1038b34–1039a2.

36. This point was brought to my attention by Hans-Georg Gadamer, whose help and inspiration I am delighted to acknowledge. For independent corroboration of the weight of this objection, one should consult the monograph on this topic by Arpe 1938. But as De Rijk (1952, pp. 14ff.) has pointed out, it is very difficult to show that either Plato or Aristotle made a sharp distinction between logical and ontological implications such as we would expect to find if they had clearly differentiated between the copulative and existential 'is.' The absence of these distinctions even in Aristotle tends to support my interpretive approach that takes logical considerations to have direct ontological implications.

37. (a) Priority in time; cf. *Phaed.* 82B2, 87C3, *Rep.* 516C–D, et al. (b) Priority in order of inquiry; cf. *Rep.* 485B6, *Theaet.* 200C–D, *Phil.* 33C8–9, *Tim.* 48E. (c) Priority in order of generation and excellence; cf. *Parm.* 155A8–B2, *Tim.* 34C. (d) Priority of a principle (ἀρχή); cf. *Phaedr.* 245C5, *Tim.* 29B–D, 29E–30A. (e) Priority in being vs. priority in speech; cf. *Tim.* 34C, *Laws* 895B.

2. The Senses of Priority in the *Categories*

1. Most Aristotelian scholars give an early date to the *Categories* relative to other works in the corpus; cf. Ackrill 1963, p. 69, and Apostle 1980, p. 1. One dissenter from this view is Furth (1978, p. 632, n. 8), who takes it to be "a mature rather than a juvenile production." Though he does not further elaborate upon the evidence for a later dating of the *Categories,* I gather that he views it as being roughly contemporaneous with the central books of the *Metaphysics.* It has often been noted that the third part (i.e. the so-called Postpraedicamenta) is only loosely connected with the previous parts but, as Ackrill points out, there is no reason to doubt its authenticity; cf. also Waitz 1844, vol. 1, pp. 316ff. In an unpublished manuscript on Aristotle's philosophical development, John Rist has conjectured that chapters 10–15 have a later date of composition closer to that of *De Interpretatione.* With reference to chapters 12–13, however, I will argue that there is strong evidence against such a conjecture. On doubts about the authenticity of the *Categories* see De Rijk 1951, pp. 129–59, and 1952, and Frede 1983, pp. 1–29.

2. For instance, the correlative opposite of πρότερον appears to be ἅμα rather than ὕστερον, even though Philoponus (*In Cat.* 194,28ff. (Busse)) claims that 'posterior' is implicit in every sense of 'priority' because these are simultaneous predicates that belong to the class of relatives. But I cannot see much evidence for this claim in the *Categories,* where Aristotle had ample opportunity to list 'prior' and 'posterior' as examples of relatives in chapter 7, if he conceived of them thus. On the contrary, he says that relatives seem to be simultaneous by nature (ἅμα τῇ φύσει) for the most part, with some notable exceptions; cf. *Cat.* 7b15ff. I shall return to these exceptions later because they are important for my interpretation of priority.

3. This peculiar fact was noted by some of the Greek commentators but none of them manages to give what I would consider a satisfactory explanation. For instance, Olympiodorus is clearly puzzled about how Aristotle could have failed to list the priorities previously established in the categories of substance and of relatives; cf. *In Cat.* 143,25ff. (Busse). Simplicius tries to deal with this puzzle by claiming that, since Aristotle had already dealt with priority in respect to substance and relatives, he does not need to deal with these senses when he treats the topic in chapters 12 and 13; cf. *In Cat.* 418,20ff. (Kalbfleisch). In the course of this chapter I will show that this explanation is inadequate.

4. I am convinced by M. Frede's (1981, pp. 1–24) well-considered claim that Aristotle uses the word κατηγορία in the sense of predication or kind of predication rather than in the sense of predicate.

5. *Cat.* 5, 2a11–19: translation by Ackrill 1963. While it may be conceded that the distinction between primary and secondary substance is not exactly the same as that between prior and posterior things, yet it is difficult to escape the conclusion that Aristotle is establishing a certain order among substances that is not included in his survey of senses of priority.

6. In his commentary on the *Categories,* Philoponus claims that substance is prior by nature (τῇ φύσει) and cites the criterion of nonreciprocal dependence to prove his point; cf. *In Cat.* 49,13–16 (Busse). Presumably he means that substance is prior to the other categories because such attributes are dependent upon some subject. When he tries to explain the distinction between primary and secondary substance, however, Philoponus appeals to the distinction between what is prior to us and what is prior by nature; cf. *In Cat.* 50,9–10. But there

is no evidence in Aristotle's text that he has any such distinction in mind and Philoponus may be simply trying to reconcile the view of substance in the *Categories* with that found in other works; cf. *In Cat.* 50,23ff. (Busse).

7. While reading both ancient and modern commentators on the *Categories,* I was struck by the fact none of the moderns noticed these inconsistencies, whereas some of the ancients were troubled by them.

8. *Cat.* 14a26–15a12: this translation of mine owes a great deal to those of Ackrill and Apostle, but I think that my differences with them justify a new translation. The text of chapters 12 and 13 is given here at the suggestion of an anonymous reader who felt that it might help to clarify the subsequent discussion. In this and all my other translations I follow the convention of placing in brackets [ ] any part of the text that is questioned by modern editors of the Aristotelian corpus. By contrast, I use parentheses ( ) to insert words or phrases that I take to be implicit in the text and that will make the translation smoother.

9. The Greek word is διάγραμμα, but this seems to be ambiguous in Greek mathematical usage between 'diagram' (cf. *De Cael.* I, 10, 279b34–35) and 'proposition' (cf. *An. Pr.* I,24, 41b13–22). Since postulates are required to license constructions, just as much as to give proofs, it would appear that either translation can serve to make the point, but I have chosen the one which I think will make it most obvious.

10. I am indebted to my colleague, Arthur Madigan, S.J., for this suggestion as to how σχεδόν might be rendered most faithfully. As Frede (1983, pp. 1–29) has rightly noted, its combination with ἀλλοτριώτατος is only partially paralleled at *Cat.* 15b28–29, and this use of the superlative along with τρόπος is without parallel in the Aristotelian corpus.

11. At Madigan's prompting, I have used "earlier-later" as a more natural translation of πρότερον καὶ ὕστερον within a temporal context, though it is merely a particularized form of the "prior-posterior" distinction.

12. This whole sentence is bracketed by Minio-Paluello (1949) but Waitz (1846, p. ii) does not seem to advert to the difficulty, which may be stated as follows: While the Greek syntax seems to suggest that these three are being treated as examples of species (εἴδη) that result from further divisions of the genus 'animal,' this can hardly be correct because they were also used to illustrate the higher divisions of the genus. Furthermore, "the footed" does not identify a distinct species of animal that travels on land, any more than "the aquatic" names a single species of fish. If we accept the brackets inserted by Minio-Paluello, however, we may take the continuative οὖν at 15a3 as pointing back to 15a1 and as summarizing the conclusion that was reached there. I am grateful to Arthur Madigan for the latter suggestion.

13. Simplicius (*In Cat.* 418,24–26) has the same impression, although he thinks that Aristotle's five ways can be extended to cover all the senses of priority listed by Strato of Lampsacus in his monograph entitled "On the Prior and the Posterior" (Περὶ τοῦ προτέρου καὶ ὑστέρου); cf. *In Cat.* 423,1ff. (Kalbfleisch). Philippe (1969, pp. 48–50) thinks that the various senses of priority in the *Categories* are distinguished according to the different modes of causality. While this interesting suggestion contains a certain grain of truth, it seems to be overly schematic because only one of these 'ways' is explicitly linked with causation by Aristotle.

14. It is difficult to say whether κυριώτατος should be taken to indicate some theoretical statement by Aristotle or merely his attempt to record the most literal meaning of prior/posterior in the Greek language. Perhaps these would not be exclusive options in his mind if he were trying to establish the focal meaning of these terms, yet there is little evidence of such an attempt in the *Categories*. The major difficulty about interpreting prior and posterior as πρὸς ἕν equivocals, however, is that Aristotle seems to change his mind about their strictest or most basic senses. For instance, in *Physics* Delta 11, he claims that the prior and the posterior belong primarily to place (τὸ δὴ πρότερον καὶ ὕστερον ἐν τόπῳ πρῶτόν ἐστιν) by virtue of position (τῇ θέσει); cf. 219a14–16. It is only at third remove, as it were, that one can speak about the prior and the posterior in time because, according to Aristotle, time always follows a motion and motion, in turn, depends upon continuous magnitude. I shall return to this passage in chapter 3, where I discuss priority with respect to place, as it is outlined in *Metaphys-*

ics Delta 11. Simplicius (*In Cat.* 419,8–20) obviously thinks that 'priority' is a *pros hen* equivocal, but he is also puzzled as to how its principal meaning can be with respect to time. He conjectures that it may be linguistic custom that has made this sense more familiar and hence 'first' in common usage from Homer onward.

15. τῷ γὰρ τὸν χρόνον πλείω εἶναι—*Cat.* 14a28–29.

16. In spite of the confidence with which Philippe (1969, p. 52) gives his schematic interpretation, I do not find it "easy to see" how priority in time as presented in the *Categories* can be reduced to priority in knowledge according to its genetic aspect. As far as I can see, Aristotle is merely recording the simplest linguistic meaning of 'prior' and 'posterior.' In *Categories* 6 he treats time as a continuous quantity whose parts do not have position relative to each other because they do not remain (ὑπομένει) but rather have a certain order (τάξιν τινὰ) by virtue of the fact that one is prior and the other is posterior in time (τῷ τὸ μὲν πρότερον εἶναι τοῦ χρόνου τὸ δ᾽ ὕστερον); cf. 5a26–30.

17. It is noteworthy that ἅμα is being treated as the contrary of both πρότερον and ὕστερον, which are correlative possibilities for things (or events) that are not simultaneous.

18. With reference to Aristotle's early notions of teleology, one should consult an interesting fragment from the *Protrepticus* (cf. Iambl. *Comm. Math.* 26) that talks about the recent and great advances of the precise sciences: "Yet these studies make most advance because they have a natural precedence; for that which is later in coming to be is prior in essence and perfection" (ἀλλ᾽ ὅμως ἐπιδίδωσι πλεῖστον, διότι τῇ φύσει ἐστὶ πρεσβύτατα· τὸ γὰρ τῇ γενέσει ὕστερον οὐσία καὶ τελειότητι προηγεῖται); cf. 83. 19–22 (Festa). What this passage seems to suggest is that Aristotle is following Plato in connecting teleology with priority in honor and perfection, in contrast to priority in time; cf. *Tim.* 34C.

19. τὸ μὴ ἀντιστρέφον κατὰ τὴν τοῦ εἶναι ἀκολούθησιν—*Cat.* 14a30.

20. Aristotle reports that the Platonists did not posit a general Idea for any schema of things in which there is a prior and a posterior; cf. *Met.* 999a6–10. Ordinal numbers are explicitly mentioned as an example of such a schema, but I think we can add to this the schema of point, line, plane, solid. Plato would have a stronger case for refusing to posit a Form in this case because it is quite likely that there was no general Greek term for quantity until Aristotle invented that category. On the issue see A. C. Lloyd 1962,pp. 67–90.

21. ὥστε οὐκ ἀντιστρέφει ἀπὸ τοῦ ἑνὸς ἡ ἀκολούθησις τοῦ εἶναι τὸ λοιπὸν—*Cat.* 14a34–35.

22. But this is precisely the sort of implication Rist (MS p. 429) denies as following from Aristotle's statement about the priority of the genus over the species, since he claims that this does not conflict with what is said in chapter 5 about the species being more substantial than the genus on the grounds that the former is more informative about primary substance. I think he fails to realize that the conceptual contexts are quite different in both places, since *Categories* 5 presupposes a subject-predicate relation between the species and the genus, whereas Platonic division forms the background for chapter 13. Of course, one might still object that, insofar as species and genera have the status of Forms, Plato's theory would prohibit one from being prior (or more real) than another, since such a relationship holds only between Forms and their instantiations. This objection points up a conflict between what we know of the theory of Forms and what Aristotle reports as being the characteristic doctrine of Platonism.

23. Simplicius (*In Cat.* 419,33ff.) accepts this as the conclusion of any argument that applies the criterion of nonreciprocal dependence and he thinks that this kind of priority is opposed to the simultaneity by nature of corresponding divisions within the same genus; cf. *In Cat.* 424,24ff. (Kalbfleisch).

24. ὅσα ἀντιστρέφει μὲν κατὰ τὴν τοῦ εἶναι ἀκολούθησιν, μηδαμῶς δὲ αἴτιον θάτερον θατέρῳ τοῦ εἶναι ἐστιν—*Cat.* 14b27–29.

25. Aristotle uses the same language of reciprocation with reference to the category of relatives when he says that they all are spoken of in relation to correlatives that reciprocate (πάντα δὲ τὰ πρός τι πρὸς ἀντιστρέφοντα λέγεται); cf. *Cat.* 6b28. He also says that relatives seem to be simultaneous by nature (ἅμα τῇ φύσει); e.g. the double is simultaneous with the half, like the master with the slave; cf. *Cat.* 7b15. The reason for this is that these correlative

pairs mutually destroy each other (συναναιρεῖ δὲ ταῦτα ἄλληλα), since if there is not a double then there is not a half. Here the language of reciprocal destruction should be seen in contrast to the criterion of priority that appeals to nonreciprocal dependence.

26. One of the *Protrepticus* fragments previously cited (cf. Iambl. *Protr.* 6, 37.26–41.5 (Pistelli)) seems to indicate that priority determines the direction of causality when it says: αἴτια τε μᾶλλον τὰ πρότερα τῶν ὑστέρων· ἐκείνων γὰρ ἀναιρουμένων ἀναιρεῖται τὰ τὴν οὐσίαν ἐξ ἐκείνων ἔχοντα.

27. πρότερον εἰκότως τῇ φύσει λέγοιτ' ἄν—*Cat.* 14a12–13.

28. My claim is supported by another passage from Aristotle's treatment of the category of relatives, where he notes an exception to the general rule that all correlatives are simultaneous by nature, citing as an example the object of knowledge that is thought to be prior to knowledge (τὸ γὰρ ἐπιστητὸν τῆς ἐπιστήμης πρότερον ἂν δόξειεν εἶναι); cf. *Cat.* 7b23–24. But he appears to think of this as priority in time when he explains that most things exist before we acquire knowledge of them, since it is very rare to see both the object of knowledge and knowledge coming into being simultaneously; cf. *Cat.* 7b24–27. Yet when the criterion of nonreciprocal dependence is applied to this pair of correlatives, they also provide an illustration of priority by nature; cf. *Cat.* 7b27–30. Thus examples of the fifth 'way' of priority are drawn from the category of relatives in the special case where one of a pair of correlatives is the cause of the other.

29. Ackrill 1963, pp. 111–12.

30. In fact, Aristotle records and adopts a distinctively Platonic meaning of 'truth' as 'true being'; cf. *Met.* 1024b17–26, 983b3, 993b30–31; *Rhet.* 1364b9, 1375b3–6; *Pol.* 1297a11.

31. περὶ γὰρ σύνθεσιν καὶ διαίρεσιν ἐστι τὸ ψεῦδος καὶ τὸ ἀληθές—*De Int.* 16a12–13.

32. For parallel passages, see *Met.* 1051b3–6; *An. Pst.* 78a27ff., 98a35ff.; *Soph. El.* 167b1ff.

33. Anton (1957, pp. 60–61) finds here a relationship between contrariety and truth that involves another application of the priority of substance. In fact, he thinks that this whole passage (*Cat.* 14b14–20) may indicate the reason why Aristotle makes first substances prior to secondary substances, since it presupposes the distinction between the grammatical and the ontological subject. As a subject-in-process, only the latter is completely real and is thus a first substance. While this may provide a plausible interpretation of *Categories* 5, there is little evidence for such distinctions in chapter 12–13. A better parallel would seem to be chapter 7 (7b27ff.), which implies that the knowable object causes knowledge in the soul, just as the perceptible object causes perception in the animal.

34. Simplicius (*In Cat.* 421,5–10) seems to think of it as a case of efficient causality analogous to the case of the father/son relation where the father is the cause of the son as maker (ὡς ποιητικόν). But I do not think that the analogy is exact because father and son belong to the same order of being, as it were, whereas the same is not true of the thing and the knowledge of it. The latter relationship is more similar to that between Forms and their particular instantiations, when the direction of causality has been reversed. In the *Hippias Major* (297Bff.), for instance, the father/son relation is introduced as a model for a putative causal relation between the Fine and the Good. But the argument ends in *aporia* perhaps because this is the wrong model for the relationship between Forms, whereas it is arguably the right one for the relationship between Forms and their instantiations.

35. One might entertain Anton's conjecture that this sense of natural priority foreshadows the relationship between primary and secondary substance but there are a number of difficulties. Apart from the fact that Aristotle does not call this relationship "natural priority," there is the difficulty of seeing how one could talk about truth with reference to the typical example of secondary substance; i.e. 'man' or 'animal.' According to Aristotle's criteria, neither of these constitutes a statement-making sentence and hence truth is not an appropriate epithet. So it would seem that the relationship between primary and secondary substance is not an instance of natural priority in the precise sense that he outlines in the *Categories*. In order to make it fit exactly, one would be forced to assume that secondary substances are not themselves things (πράγματα) but concepts in the mind that may somehow be called "true accounts." But this conflicts with Aristotle treatment of 'man' and 'animal' as things, primarily,

and only secondarily as terms and concepts. Of course, as Brentano (1862 and 1975, pp. 17ff.) points out, there are derivative senses of 'truth' in Aristotle; e.g. as applied to things; cf. *Met.* V, 29, 1024b17–26. But for things in which there is no combination or separation (i.e. for simple things), 'truth' is grasping or uttering, while 'falsity' is ignorance; cf. *De Int.* 4, 16b28.

36. It may be significant that in *Categories* 13 Aristotle does not list any meanings of 'simultaneous' that might directly correspond with either of the last two meanings of priority. This lack of correspondence stimulated Greek commentators like Iamblichus and Simplicius to great feats of imaginative reconstruction in redressing the balance. It does not seem to have occurred to them that perhaps Aristotle did not find any common meanings of 'simultaneous' in Greek usage that might plausibly be opposed to priority in order or priority in value. Indeed, the fact that the notions of order and value seem to be incompatible with simultaneity may help to explain why the latter concept drops out of sight in *Metaphysics* Delta 11.

37. καθάπερ ἐπὶ τῶν ἐπιστημῶν καὶ τῶν λόγων—*Cat.* 14a36–37.

38. This linguistic connection is confirmed at *Metaphysics* Beta 3, 998a20–31. Cf. also LSJ., p. 1647.

39. Simplicius, on the contrary, thinks that this example does not give us the principal (κυρίως) meaning of priority but only the sense with reference to order. His argument seems to be that the principal sense is causal priority (as in the fifth meaning), whereas an introduction is not the cause of a narrative but only precedes it in order; cf. *In Cat.* 420,16–19 (Kalbfleisch).

40. It is rather odd that Aristotle should demote priority with respect to order into such an insignificant place in his whole treatment of priority. One might object (as Donald Morrison has done in personal conversation) that *every* sense of priority is with respect to some order, given the very nature of the concept. But perhaps that is the reason why priority with respect to some order is given a strict and narrow sense, so that other special senses of priority can be distinguished. If Aristotle simply used the generic sense, he would be depriving himself of all the subtle distinctions that enable him to distance himself from Platonism.

41. Simplicius thinks that it indicates a departure from customary usage, since not everyone uses the term 'prior' for the best and most honored, even though they are prior by nature just as the gods are prior to mortals; cf. *In Cat.* 420,20ff. (Kalbfleisch). But this seems to conflict with the plain sense of what Aristotle says about this being ordinary usage and hence being philosophically the most inappropriate meaning of priority. As a good Neoplatonist, of course, Simplicius *knows* that he must reconcile this with what Aristotle says elsewhere about the priority of the divine life as better and more honorable than human life.

42. I cannot find any clear evidence for the claim of Philippe (1969, p. 50 n. 200) that Aristotle is thinking of the final cause when he outlines this fourth sense of priority. On the contrary, the language used here is without parallel in other works like the *Physics* and *Metaphysics* that deal with the many senses of cause.

43. Simplicius refuses to accept the reported claim of Iamblichus that priority with respect to substance has been left out of the senses of priority in the *Categories*. Instead, he claims that it is included under the fourth sense of priority according to the more honorable and the best; cf. *In Cat.* 421,22–24. But it is very difficult to see how this claim can be justified on the basis of Aristotle's text, even though the fourth 'way' is called priority in nature.

44. This solution might also explain why some ancient commentators who insist upon the title 'Categories' found in the 'Postpraedicamenta' some material that seemed alien to the purpose of the whole treatise and that seemed more fitting for an introduction to the *Topics;* cf. Ammon. *In Cat.* 14,18ff. and Simpl. *In Cat.* 379,8ff. Yet, my proposal should not be taken to imply that the 'Postpraedicamenta' has no place in the project of the whole *Categories*. On the contrary, I agree with Frede (1983, pp. 1–29) that it represents a genuine part of a work that is rather loosely unified as an inquiry into the different senses of important philosophical concepts, just as in the case of *Metaphysics* Delta. But Frede seems not to have noticed the inconsistency between chapters 5 and 12, which tends to undermine efforts to give the whole work any systematic coherence.

45. *Categories* 2b17–21: translation by Ackrill 1963.

46. τὰ μὲν γὰρ γένη κατὰ τῶν εἰδῶν κατηγορεῖται, τὰ δὲ εἴδη κατὰ τῶν γενῶν οὐκ ἀντιστρέφει—*Cat.* 2b20–21.

47. This passage provides some vital evidence for Donald Morrison's claim that, in spite of his break with Platonism, Aristotle still continued to accept some version of Plato's "degrees-of-reality" thesis. I think that most of the talk about natural priority in the *Categories* can be seen to support a weaker version of this thesis as synonymous with the ordering of beings; cf. 2a11–12, 2b7–27, 3b33–4a9. By contrast, Morrison thinks there is firm evidence for what he calls the "intensity interpretation," which, among other things, maintains that there is a real inference from priority in substance to a greater degree of substance.

3. The Senses of Priority in *Metaphysics* Delta

1. Reale (1980, ch. 8) dissents from the standard view that Book Delta is merely a philosophical lexicon, and he tries to justify its present position in the *Metaphysics* in terms of Aristotle's overall plan for a science of metaphysics. Furthermore, he argues, Delta cannot serve as a metaphysical lexicon because of its incomplete state; i.e. it does not cover all the important metaphysical concepts. But it is not obvious to me that Aristotle ever set out to give a complete list of all his principal metaphysical terms. Since Delta is frequently referred to by means of the title "On the Many Senses" (περὶ τοῦ ποσαχῶς), I think it is more plausible to take this book as covering only those terms whose usage involves many different meanings.

2. At *Physics* A 6 (189b23ff.) we find a revealing argument to the effect that primary contrarieties cannot be many because "substance" (οὐσία) is a single genus of being and so the principles can differ in priority and posteriority (πρότερον καὶ ὕστερον) but not in genus. The reason given is that in a single genus there can be only one contrariety and all other contrarieties (in that genus) are thought to be referred to one (ἀνάγεσθαι δοκοῦσιν εἰς μίαν). There is an interesting hint here that the priority and posteriority among contrarieties may depend on this logical characteristic of referring to one central meaning; i.e. their *pros hen* structure.

3. It has been objected (again by Donald Morrison, who read an earlier draft of this monograph) that Aristotle does not appear to be following his categories in any systematic way here. Such an objection is deflected somewhat by the fact that Alexander (*In Metaph.* 384,33ff.) still talks about the "genera" in which there is priority and posteriority, even though he contrasts this treatment of priority with that found in the *Categories*. I would argue that some of these genera obviously belong in the list of categories and that Aristotle is conducting his inquiry within that general framework, even though not all of the categories contain entities that have prior/posterior relations. In support of my argument, I would defer to the authority of Simplicius (*In Cat.* 422,25–30) who thinks that the listed five ways of priority fit under the so-called highest genera. Aristotle's use of the term "genera" as synonymous with his categories is well attested; cf. *Phy.* 189a14, 189b24; *De Caelo* 312a13. Cf. also Bonitz 1870, p. 152a16ff.

4. I am accepting the addition of εἶναι by Ross and Jaeger because it has a clear parallel in 1018b12.

5. Jaeger has bracketed τοῦ νῦν in his text but I follow Ross in accepting these words, which parallel b17.

6. I think that the aorist participle (χρησαμένων) used here as a genitive absolute gives the whole state of affairs a temporal index that is necessary if 'the now' is to serve its purpose as a principle with reference to which earlier and later can be established.

7. It is difficult to ascertain the referent of αὕτη but it can hardly be παῖς or ἀνδρός, which are both masculine nouns. Thus it must be either κίνησις or some implicit referent like γένεσις. See my discussion of this point below.

8. By translating τὸ ὕστερον as "the inferior" here, I am not being strictly consistent, but I think that the personal and social character of the example warrants the suggestion of a so-

cial hierarchy, where the superior makes a decision that must be obeyed by the inferior. As with 'before' and 'after' in the case of time, this is another one of those particular applications of the prior/posterior distinction.

9. My translation of λόγος as "account" is an attempt to remain neutral on whether this sense is identical with priority in definition or whether it is merely priority in formula. Such a general term as "account" can cover both of these senses, which I take to be included under the heading of priority in knowledge.

10. Cf. *An. Pst.* I, 4, for the criteria that determine when something is a *per se* attribute of its subject.

11. Aquinas thinks that all five senses can be brought under priority with respect to quantity, either in continuous or discrete forms; cf. *In Metaph.* V, L. 13, c. 937. Since there is little support for such an interpretation in Delta 11, he is obviously relying on what Aristotle says in *Physics* IV about the priority of magnitude to motion. This is a strategy that I also use to elucidate the meanings of priority in Delta, but I am not convinced that the Thomist interpretation makes full sense of the extant text, although it is always worth noting.

12. Alexander is also convinced that a principle of location determined by nature must be something like the center or extremity of the universe; cf. *In Metaph.* 385, 11ff. (Hayduck). Aquinas concurs and offers, by way of example, two different orderings of the four elements depending on whether we take the center or the boundary as a first principle with respect to place; cf. *In Metaph.* L. 13, c. 938.

13. Aristotle accepts the Platonic view that the universe has the geometrical shape of a perfect sphere, which has only two clearly defined places as opposites, i.e. the center and circumference; cf. *De Caelo* II, 4 and *Timaeus* 33Bff.

14. *Phy.* IV, 11, 219a14–19: translation by Apostle (1969), who is overtranslating when he characterizes the prior and the posterior as "attributes" of a place. Logically, prior and posterior are contrary attributes of being, and consequently, entities that are spatially ordered with reference to a determinate principle are prior and posterior. It is only indirectly, therefore, that the prior and the posterior could be called attributes of place. Philippe (1969, p. 49) thinks that this kind of priority should be understood in the sense of position, whereas if the previous and the consequent (as he calls them) are in magnitude, they are necessarily also in movement, by analogy with magnitude.

15. We should not fail to notice the importance of such a criterion of spatial ordering for Aristotle's hierarchical system of the physical universe, which I shall discuss briefly in my final chapter.

16. τῷ νῦν ὡς ἀρχῇ καὶ πρώτῳ χρησαμένων—*Met.* 1018b19.

17. It is not clear that such a linear concept of time is appropriate to the Greek context, but my argument works just as well with a cyclical notion because 'the now' is like an arbitrary point on a circle that can determine a prior and a posterior only if we assume the direction to be constant in the movement of time. Whether we take the linear or cyclic model of time, there seems to be no principle that is determined by nature like the center and circumference of a spherical universe; cf. Callahan 1948.

18. Alexander (*In Metaph.* 385,31–33) notes that, although 'the now' is the natural principle of time (ἀρχὴ χρόνου φύσει), it is not always the case that this principle is determined by nature (φύσει) because it seems to be constantly taken as different. I take it that only the second meaning of 'nature' here is synonymous with 'absolute,' since Alexander is referring to the manner in which the principle is determined as if it were somehow relative to us.

19. In *Categories* 6 (as I have noted in the previous chapter) Aristotle differentiates time from other continuous quantities, like place, by virtue of the fact that its parts do not endure and so do not have position; cf. 5a26–29. Therefore, even though the present moment is contiguous with both past and future (5a7–8), we must presume that for him it cannot serve as an absolute principle because it is constantly changing.

20. ὅταν ὁρίσωμεν τὴν κίνησιν, τῷ πρότερον καὶ ὕστερον ὁρίζοντες—219a22–23; cf. 219b2–3.

21. *Phy.* IV, 14, 223a4–13: translation by Apostle 1969.

22. On this point consult also *Phy.* VIII, 1, 251b10–11.

23. Perhaps Aquinas (*In Metaph.* V, L.13, c937) is correct to bring place and time under the rubric of continuous magnitude, since they are both derivative quantities. Yet that does not help us to resolve the question of whether place or time gives us the chief sense of priority, because each of them seems to have quite a different principle for determining such priority. Corish (1976, p. 251) argues that Aristotle begs the question when he tries to derive the temporal order from that of κίνησις and, ultimately, from that of μέγεθος.

24. There is some ambiguity in Aristotle's use of κίνησις as a general word for change in the *Physics*. In Book 3, chapter 1, he uses it in a sense that covers substantial change but in Book 5 he explicitly excludes this kind of change (μεταβολή) from falling under the general term for motion; i.e. κίνησις.

25. τὸ γὰρ ἐγγύτερον τοῦ πρώτου κινήσαντος πρότερον—*Met.*1018b20–21.

26. For confirmation of this point consult *Phy.* VIII, 5, 257b16ff.

27. A possible grammatical solution would be to assume that some word like γένεσις is the implicit referent of the word αὕτη when Aristotle explains that 'this' is a sort of absolute principle. Such a solution would be consistent with his general position and would also free us of the difficulty that 'this' can hardly refer to either παῖς or ἀνδρός, since the most natural way to take both is as masculine nouns. If one accepts this proposal then one should take 'boy' and 'man' as referring to the same individual at two different stages, one of which is prior with respect to change because it is closer to the primary bringer of change; i.e. the generating father. This is consistent with the statement in *Physics* Delta 14 that seems to make priority in motion dependent upon priority in time. Aquinas (*In Metaph.* V, L. 13, c. 942) gives a similar interpretation when he explains that the boy is prior to the man because he is closer to the generator, which itself is a principle in an absolute sense according to nature. But he neglects to explain how this comes under the general rubric of continuous magnitude and that is difficult to show, unless we assume that absolute generation presupposes locomotion.

28. I think that the problem of interpretation here is exacerbated by Aristotle's choice of a bad example and the brevity of his explanation. On the other hand, Alexander (*In Metaph.* 385,33ff.) treats the meaning of priority and its illustration here as being perfectly straightforward, since he devotes only seven odd lines of commentary to it. According to his interpretation, the child is prior to the man with respect to motion because it is closer to the generator (ἐγγυτέρω γὰρ τῷ γεννήσαντι); i.e. the father. Furthermore, by way of explaining Aristotle's remark about this being an absolute principle, Alexander elucidates it as a reference to a natural principle of motion that is always prior to things moved by nature. Thus, for instance, the motion of the fixed stars is prior because it is closer to the Prime Mover, just as in the sublunary realm the child is prior because it is closer to its prime mover.

29. Simplicius (*In Cat.* 422,27–28) thinks that priority with respect to power falls under the category of relatives (πρός τι), but he does not provide any detailed justification for this. Perhaps he is simply drawing this conclusion from the internal logic of the concept itself, which seems to presuppose a relation between at least two things.

30. μὴ κινοῦντός τε ἐκείνου μὴ κινεῖσθαι καὶ κινοῦντος κινεῖσθαι—*Met.* 1018b24–25.

31. I am grateful to Donald Morrison for drawing my attention to the linguistic fact that ἀρχή refers primarily to the *office* and not to the holder of the office, who would be called an ἀρχός/ἀρχών. At any rate, this does not really affect my point about the play on words because the plural ἀρχαί was commonly used to refer to leaders; cf. LSJ., pp. 252–54. Incidentally, Alexander cites the leader as his prime example of priority with respect to power; cf. *In Metaph.* 386,1ff. (Hayduck).

32. This special sense of 'power' is explicitly included under the general sense of priority with respect to potency in *Metaphysics* Theta 8; cf. LSJ., p. 452, for its archaic meaning in Homer. See also the discussion in chapter 4 of this monograph.

33. Aquinas (*In Metaph.* V,. L. 13, c. 943) also thinks that priority with respect to power can be brought under priority in motion because the one moved by the decision of the leader is posterior in motion and in power.

34. Simplicius (*In Cat.* 422,28) thinks that this particular sense of priority with respect to

order falls under the category of position (τὸ κεῖσθαι), and this is made plausible by Aristotle's examples that all seem to involve relative position. Aquinas (*In Metaph.* V, L. 13, c. 944) claims that this sense has to do with priority in discrete things, but this is not explicit in the Greek text.

35. ὅσα πρός τι ἓν ὡρισμένον διέστηκε κατά τινα λόγον—*Met.* 1018b26–27.

36. Szabo (1978, pp. 99ff.) has made a convincing connection between διάστημα and λόγος in the language of ancient musical theory and mathematics. Alexander uses as a synonym for διέστηκε the more prosaic verb ἀφέστηκε, but that does not change its basic meaning of things being set apart at intervals; cf. *In Metaph.* 386,9ff. (Hayduck).

37. By contrast, Aquinas thinks that there is a clear difference between the examples in this respect. In the ordering of the chorus, for instance, he claims that the principle taken (i.e. the chorus leader) is truly a beginning as the highest among others, just as the king stands at the apex of his realm. In the case of the lyre strings, on the other hand, Aquinas seems to suspect that there is something conventional about taking the middle string as a principle of ordering; cf. *In Metaph.* V, L. 13, c. 945. It is interesting to note that the way in which a particular thinker makes this distinction between natural and conventional ordering appears to reflect a whole world view.

38. Philippe (1969, p. 50) thinks that priority according to the order of knowledge falls under two mutually exclusive headings: (*a*) according to λόγος, which he takes to be a "conceptual ordering" of the universal before the particular and of the simple before the complex, (*b*) according to sensation, which gives priority to the individual over the universal. But the latter can hardly be priority in knowledge, strictly speaking, so it is perhaps better to talk about priority in acquaintance.

39. Cf. S. Mansion 1979, pp. 161–70.

40. This would be similar to the distinction between being part of the substantial form and being part of the composite that Aristotle elucidates in *Metaphysics* Zeta 10–11, where he develops the different senses of 'part' that are briefly outlined in Delta 25. Consult my fifth chapter for a more detailed discussion of this distinction and of how different senses of 'priority' correspond to different senses of 'part.'

41. καίτοι οὐκ ἐνδέχεται μουσικὸν εἶναι μὴ ὄντος μουσικοῦ τινός—*Met.* 1018b36–37.

42. Alexander gives a rather strange explanation of this kind of priority, which suggests that he may have been thinking of genus and species in comparison to a sensible particular. What he says is that those things that are prior with respect to definition (κατὰ τὸν λόγον) are the universals (τὰ καθόλου) that are also prior absolutely by nature (ἁπλῶς τῇ φύσει πρῶτα), since it is through these that things are known scientifically; cf. *In Metaph.* 386,27ff. (Hayduck). By contrast, the things that are prior with respect to perception (κατὰ τὴν αἴσθησιν) are the particulars (τὰ καθ' ἕκαστα) that seem to us (πρὸς ἡμᾶς) to have priority but do not have it absolutely. Now I think it is clear that Alexander is going beyond Aristotle's text here though he is hardly misrepresenting the main point of the passage. Aquinas is on safer ground when he claims that, according to Aristotle, what is intelligible *per se* (i.e. the universal) is prior in knowledge to what is only intelligible *per accidens;* cf. *In Metaph.* V, L. 13, c. 947.

43. Philippe (1969, p. 50) thinks that this represents a separate sense of priority "according to properties" (πάθη) but I cannot find any precedent for such a sense in Aristotle. Owens (1951, p. 320), on the other hand, correctly points out that only three different classes of priority are outlined in Delta 11.

44. *Met.* V, 11, 1018b37–1019a1: translation (and italics) by Apostle 1966.

45. Aquinas (*In Metaph.* V, L. 13, c. 949) groups this sense of priority under the general rubric of priority in knowledge while relying on the explicit assumption that lines are naturally (naturaliter) prior to surfaces. Alexander, by contrast, takes this sense of priority to be governed by the subsequent Platonic criterion that he assumes to be added by way of clarifying the meaning; cf. *In Metaph.* 386,38ff. (Hayduck). But this is not totally incompatible with my grouping, since such a criterion was also used by the Platonists to determine priority in knowledge, as we have seen from the *Topics.*

46. Cf. *An. Pst.* I, 4, 73a35ff. and 5, 74a4ff.

47. *Met.* 1019a1–4: translation (and italics) by Apostle 1966.

48. Without appealing to authority, it is interesting to note that Aquinas also counts three major groupings of senses in his commentary on this chapter; cf. *In Metaph.* V, L. 13, c. 936ff. and Owens (1951, p. 320).

49. On consulting the commentary of Aquinas after I had made this connection for myself, I was pleased to find that he mentions the same criterion of priority in the *Categories* as being identical with the criterion used here; cf. *In Metaph.* V, L. 13, c. 950. I would claim, however, that the criteria are not identical though they yield very similar results.

50. ὅσα ἐνδέχεται εἶναι ἄνευ ἄλλων, ἐκεῖνα δὲ ἄνευ ἐκείνων μή—*Met.* 1019a3–4.

51. As a paraphrase for the Platonic criterion, Alexander offers the following: λέγεσθαι γάρ φησι καὶ φύσει τε καὶ οὐσία πρῶτα, ὡς τὰ συναναιροῦντα μὲν μὴ ουναναιρούμενα δέ, ᾧ φησι σημαινομένῳ πρώτῳ Πλάτωνα χρήσασθαι—*In Metaph.* 387,5–7 (Hayduck). This tends to confirm the formulaic correspondences for which I argued in my first chapter.

52. Ross 1924 i, p. 317.

53. Mutschmann (1906, pp. xvii–xviii) thinks that the reference is to a collection of so-called Platonic Divisions Aristotle had to hand, but Cherniss (1944, p. 44, n. 33) casts doubt upon such a claim. On the other hand, Cherniss is not convinced by attempts like those of Ross (1924 i, pp. 160–61) and Apelt (1891, pp. 226–29) to find a definite reference to Plato's extant works, though he does concede that the distinction is used in *Timaeus* 34B–C. Klein (1968, p. 71) takes Aristotle to be referring to the important role mathematical 'hypothesis theory' plays in the *Phaedo* (99Aff.) and *Republic* (510D–E).

54. Cf. *Phaedrus* 265D–E, *Sophist* 267D.

55. As against this claim, it must be noted that Aquinas thinks Aristotle is referring to such characteristic Platonic doctrines as the priority in essence of universals over particulars, and of surfaces over bodies, and of lines over surfaces, and of number over all things; cf. *In Metaph.* V, L. 13, c. 950. But this does not appear to fit with the few references to Platonic divisions that we find in the Aristotelian corpus; cf. *de Part. Anim.* 642b10, *de Gen. Corr.* 330b15. The first of these references seems to suggest that some sort of handbook of standard divisions may have been circulated in the Academy.

56. In this passage, I think we can find some crucial evidence for the link between priority and the thesis about degrees of being within the Platonic/Aristotelian tradition, since such a criterion of priority clearly serves to establish degrees of substantiality.

57. τὰ μὲν ἄνευ σώματος ἐνδέχεσθαι δοκεῖ εἶναι τὸ δὲ σῶμα ἄνευ τούτων ἀδύνατον—*Met.* 1002a6–8.

58. ὅσα μόρια ἐνυπάρχοντά ἐστιν ἐν τοῖς τοιούτοις ὁρίζοντά τε καὶ τόδε τι σημαίνοντα, ὧν ἀναιρουμένων ἀναιρεῖται τὸ ὅλον—*Met.* 1017b20–21.

59. ἀναιρουμένου τε γὰρ οὐδὲν εἶναι, καὶ ὁρίζειν πάντα—*Met.* 1017b20–21.

60. There seems to be an internal inconsistency in a Platonic position that accepts a degrees-of-reality thesis and yet denies that any one of the Ideas is prior to any other. Perhaps it was an awareness of such apparent inconsistency that prompted Plato to explore the relationships (including priority and posteriority) between Ideas in dialogues such as the *Parmenides, Sophist* and *Statesman.*

61. *Met.* 1019a4–11: translation by Apostle 1966.

62. Aquinas fails to retain this link when, contrary to what the Greek text says, he describes this as a second way of priority with respect to order in essence (secundum ordinem in essendo); i.e. priority with respect to the order of substance and accident; cf. *In Metaph.* V, L. 13, c. 950–51. Clearly, this is not a second sense of priority but rather a first result of the priority criterion within the new context of the many senses of being.

63. τὸ ὑποκείμενον πρότερον, διὸ ἡ οὐσία πρότερον—*Met.* 1019a5–6.

64. Ross 1924 i, p. 318.

65. Alexander (*In Metaph.* 387,7ff.) also takes Aristotle to be arguing for the priority of substance on the basis of the previous criteria and paraphrases the argument as follows: "Since being is said in many ways, what is first with respect to being (κατὰ τὸ εἶναι) and sub-

sistence (κατὰ τὴν ὕπαρξιν) he calls the subject for all other things and such is substance. For insofar as it (i.e. substance) destroys them but is not itself destroyed, it is first among the others. But, insofar as it underlies while the others are in it as subject, it is especially the first thing" (my translation). Incidentally, Aquinas also takes this to be the conclusion of an argument based upon the notion of a primary and self-subsistent subject; cf. *In Metaph.* V, L. 13, c. 951.

66. Λέγεται δ' ἡ οὐσία, εἰ μὴ πλεοναχῶς, ἀλλ' ἐν τέταρσί γε μάλιστα—*Met.* 1028b33–34.

67. καθ' οὖ τὰ ἄλλα λέγεται, ἐκεῖνο δὲ αὐτὸ μηκέτι κατ' ἄλλου—*Met.* 1028b36–37.

68. Cf. *Physics* A 6 (189a30ff.) where Aristotle claims that a subject is a principle and is thought to be prior to what is predicated of it.

69. μὴ οὐσῶν οὖν τῶν πρώτων οὐσιῶν ἀδύνατον τῶν ἄλλων τι εἶναι—*Cat.* 2b3–6.

70. μάλιστα γὰρ δοκεῖ εἶναι οὐσία τὸ ὑποκείμενον πρῶτον—*Met.* 1029a1–2.

71. While the individual man, for instance, is clearly called the primary substance in *Categories* 5, I do not mean to suggest here that Aristotle never changed his mind about this being the primary sense of 'substance.' In fact, there is considerable evidence that he does so in *Metaphysics* Z–H.

72. Cf. LSJ., p. 575, which lists ἐντελέχεια as an Aristotelian coinage. Even though δύναμις is used by Plato, it does not seem to have any special technical sense, except perhaps with reference to mathematics; cf. *Theaet.* 147D, *Tim.* 54B. In the *Gorgias* (456A–C) Plato seems to be punning on the colloquial meaning of δύναμις when he uses it to refer to the subject-matter or scope of sophistic rhetoric.

73. διαλυθέντος γὰρ κατ' ἐντελέχειαν ἔσται—*Met.* 1019a10–11.

74. Cf. Ross 1924 i, p. 318.

75. Cf. Kirwan 1971, pp. 155–56.

76. It is noteworthy that the usually acute Alexander finds no such difficulty for the interpretation of this passage, which he sums up as follows: when the whole is dissolved each of these (parts) becomes separated in actuality from the whole in which they were first beings 'existing' potentially; cf. *In Metaph.* 387,25–26.

77. While I do not wish to deny that Aristotle uses εἶναι in a distinctively existential sense (as distinct from predicative or veridical senses), I do want to insist that 'existence' for him is not univocal but has many modes, even when it applies to substance. For instance, Aristotle obviously thinks that there is a difference between the modes of being of sensible and supersensible substance.

78. *Met.* 1019a11–14: translation by Apostle 1966.

79. Cf. Apostle 1966, p. 307.

80. Ross 1924 i, p. 318.

81. ὅσα ἐνδέχεται εἶναι ἄνευ ἄλλων, ἐκεῖνα δὲ ἄνευ ἐκείνων μή—*Met.* 1019a3–4. Aquinas (*In Metaph.* V, L.13, c. 953) also thinks that all the senses of priority can be reduced to this way, although he concedes that Aristotle's reduction refers to all these last ways of natural and substantial priority.

82. Cf. *In Metaph.* 387,32–388,39 (Hayduck).

4. The Focal Sense of Priority

1. I recognize that I am making a host of undefended assumptions here, but I think it is arguable that Theta 8 represents a more developed discussion of priority than what we have found in Delta 11 and in *Categories* 12. For one thing, there is the well-recognized fact that the theory of potency and actuality is Aristotle's own unique contribution to the Greek philosophical tradition, and such terminology does not feature in what are acknowledged to be his earlier works. Grayeff (1974, p. 203) notes that this whole chapter represents the most extreme form of Peripatetic teleology and he assigns it a very late date; i.e. the last decade of

the fourth century. Though one need not accept such conjectures about additions made by subsequent Peripatetic lectures, it is clear that Theta 8 is a very late treatise in the Aristotelian corpus.

2. I am not translating the words bracketed by Ross and Jaeger as a possible corruption of the text. In his commentary on Theta 1, Ross (1924 ii, p. 240) notes that, although Aristotle distinguishes two senses of δύναμις that may be rendered by 'power' and 'potentiality,' he fails to preserve the distinction systematically.

3. Reading τοῦ λόγου with Jaeger at 1049b17 on the authority of Alexander's paraphrase.

4. Ross (1924 ii, pp. 262–63) notes the difficulty of the Greek here and conjectures that the words ἢ ὅτι οὐδὲν δεόνται θεωρεῖν may be a gloss, even though Alexander seems to have read all the words except ὅτι. Out of the three possible readings suggested by Ross, I find the first most plausible but yet it does not make complete sense of the text as we have it. Grayeff (1974, p. 199) makes the implausible suggestion that the word ὡδί points to some table of concepts and their opposites that is used to illustrate the artificial and unnecessary character of speculation by students.

5. Ross (1924 ii, pp. 262–63) thinks that Alexander's conjecture about this being a reference to a remarkable sculpture must be wrong because Pauson is reputed to have been a painter. Thus, going by the historical evidence, he thinks the best conjecture is that Aristotle is referring to some kind of trick picture like the one of a horse running, which also represents a horse rolling on its back when turned upside down. Grayeff (1974, p. 199) thinks the point of the reference is that from one angle the Hermes is hidden in his case but is visible from another angle.

6. For the sake of consistency in translation I continue to render ἐνέργεια as "actuality," though perhaps "activity" might better serve Aristotle's linguistic point here (it is certainly better at 1050a34–b1). His etymological analysis appears to hinge on the parallel in linguistic structure between the words ἐνέργεια and ἐντέλεχεια, which both involve the same abstract conceptualization based upon the concrete words ἔργον and τέλος, respectively. But it is almost impossible to capture this word play in ordinary English and so I have tried for the plain sense of the Greek.

7. Even though 'use' is the literal meaning of χρῆσις, I think it may have instrumental connotations that are inappropriate to Aristotle's point; i.e. that the faculty of sight has no other goal than its own exercise.

8. This is a translation of ἔργον, which I have also rendered as 'product' in the previous passage for the sake of consistency, even though there I think that 'work' fits the linguistic context better.

9. It is difficult to capture in translation the formal contrast between the more and the less (μᾶλλον... ἧττον) that one can find in the Greek, though one can get the general gist of the comparison between activities like seeing, which are nothing less than their own goal, and activities like housebuilding, whose goal is something more than the capacity for building. I am grateful to Arthur Madigan for his insightful suggestions about this and other difficult passages.

10. This is still consistent with his definition of motion as the *activity* of the potential qua potential; cf. *Phy.* 201a10–11.

11. Cf. *Met.* 1049b5–8 and 1019a15–18. This is identified in Theta 1 as the primary and "strictest" (μάλιστα κυρίως) sense of potency, which might be identified as a "power" or the source of change in another thing (or what we might call an efficient cause); cf. *Met.* 1045b35ff. By contrast, the "potentiality" (δύναμις) of the same thing qua itself to move toward some goal or engage in some activity seems more akin to the final cause.

12. But in his summary of Strato's book about priority and posteriority, Simplicius claims that the priority of the incomplete over the complete can be reduced to priority with respect to time, since the end is the last stage (ἐσχάτον) in everything; cf. *In Cat.* 423, 1ff. (Kalbfleisch). In spite of the authority of this tradition, however, I cannot find any evidence for the presence of a final cause in Aristotle's treatment of priority in time either in the *Categories* or in *Metaphysics* Delta.

13. Ross (1924 ii, p. 260) does not think that Aristotle has proved his point; i.e. that there must be an actual member of the species prior in time to the potential member. Ross argues that this is not proved by pointing out that an actual member is needed to transform the potential member into an actual member. Aristotle would have proved his point, according to Ross, if he had referred to the female parent who provides the matter rather than to the male parent who only transforms the matter. Presumably, on account of Aristotle's anti-Platonism, Ross does not think that the species form can be treated as an ultimate and primary cause that might stop the infinite temporal regress that could occur if some potency comes before every actuality.

14. Grayeff (1974, p. 200) also thinks that the conundrum is Megaric in origin but that it was wielded by later Sceptics against the Peripatetic doctrine of identity in form of the actual and the potential. For this and other reasons he makes the implausible suggestion that much of the chapter is the product of post-Aristotelian lecturers within the Lyceum.

15. This is already implied in the introduction to Theta, where Aristotle refers to the primacy of substance over the other categories and speaks of the need to correlate the categorial senses of being with the major distinction between potential and actual being; cf. *Met.* 1045b27ff.

16. This passage seems to involve both the material and moving cause, which can also be expressed in terms of priority. With reference to material causality, one might say that potency is prior in time to actuality on the level of the individual thing. At the specific level, however, activity is prior in time to potency because one member of a species is the moving cause of another.

17. τὰ τῆ γενέσει ὕστερα τῷ εἴδει καὶ τῆ οὐσίᾳ πρότερα—*Met.* 1050a4–5.

18. In fact, it is necessary to distinguish between the species and the individual levels so as to remove the apparent inconsistency between the previous claim that actuality is prior to potency in generation and the present claim that it is prior in substance because it is posterior in generation. Grayeff (1974, p. 200) may be correct in thinking that originally there were two different views on the relationship of actuality to potentiality in time, but he seems too intent on textual archaeology to notice that Aristotle tries to reconcile such tensions within a single view.

19. ἅπαν ἐπ᾽ ἀρχὴν βαδίζει τὸ γιγνόμενον καὶ τέλος—*Met.* 1050a7–8.

20. Cf. *De Cael.* 271a33, 291b14; *De Part. An.* 658a9, 661b24; *De Gen. An.* 741b5, 744a36; *Pol.* 1256b21.

21. This set of correspondence shows us how Aristotle might find it plausible to reduce one to the other and even treat them as being interchangeable; e.g. by treating the material aspect as a potency for the form, which is therefore taken as the activity; cf. *Met.* 1050b2.

22. Thus Aristotle's general definition of change is "the activity of the potency qua potency"; cf. *Phy.* III, 1, 201a10–15, a27–29, 201b4–5.

23. Perhaps this can be correlated with the distinction made in Theta 6 between movement (κίνησις) and action (πρᾶξις) in terms of whether or not its goal is contained in itself; cf. *Met.* 1048b18ff. Among examples of movement, in this sense, is housebuilding because its goal is a product external to the activity; whereas it is characteristic of actions like seeing and thinking to be self-fulfilling at every instant; i.e. to see is already to have seen.

24. Grayeff (1974, p. 200) finds signs of Stoic influence in the references to the activity of the soul and the happy life, but I see no reason to look further than *Metaphysics* Lambda for this interweaving of ethics and metaphysics. In fact, as Grayeff acknowledges, the subsequent argument for a Prime Mover as an ultimate actuality seems to point toward Lambda 8.

25. Grayeff (1974, p. 201) takes this word to be of later Hellenistic usage and conjectures that the whole clause may have been supplied by some librarian-editor who fitted the material together. Even if that were correct, however, it would not undermine my claim that for Aristotle eternal entities are prior in substance to corruptible entities because they have a greater degree of reality.

26. Grayeff (1974, p. 200) sees this part of the chapter as being "scientific-physical" in character, as distinct from the "eidetic-teleological" discussion in the central part. As evi-

dence for this, he points out that the priority of actuality over potentiality is no longer debated, but only the priority of eternal over perishable substances. But I am not convinced that this distinction holds up against Aristotle's claim that eternal things are actualities that are prior in substance to corruptible things precisely because they do not have potency in any absolute sense.

27. By contrast, Reale (1980, pp. 221ff.) finds the theological component of first philosophy present in Theta but he seems to be extrapolating rather than citing precise textual evidence.

28. It is possible that here we see Aristotle beginning to develop his mature conception of 'priority' as a πρὸς ἕν equivocal with pure actuality (or separated substantial form) as the focal meaning. Such speculation tends to be confirmed by his descriptions of the Prime Mover as pure actuality and by his arguments for its priority, some of which I will examine in the last chapter.

5. Getting the Priorities Right

1. πρῶτον ὂν τὸ τί ἐστι, ὅπερ σημαίνει τὴν οὐσίαν—*Met.* 1028a14–15.

2. This assumption is an integral part of the famous turn to the *logoi* that is reported in Socrates' fictional autobiography in the *Phaedo* (96Aff.) and that determined the character of Platonic/Aristotelian inquiry about nature; cf. Gadamer 1978, ch. 1.

3. Throughout this passage we find the word μᾶλλον being used frequently and this might lead us to suspect that some version of the degrees-of-being thesis lurks in the background. In spite of this, however, Morrison (1987) concludes that Aristotle is not here talking about degrees of being because μᾶλλον is consistently linked with verbs of appearing rather than with existential verbs.

4. *Met.* VII, 3, 1028a31–b4: translation by Apostle 1966.

5. As I have noted in a previous chapter, one obstacle to such a claim is that Aristotle seems to change his mind about the principal meaning of priority between the *Categories* and the *Physics.* We might conjecture that, in the latter text, the need to establish that locomotion is the primary kind of motion may be responsible for the emphasis placed on priority with respect to place. In *Metaphysics* Theta, however, he seems to assign the principal meaning of priority to substance as pure actuality. Yet these different assignments are compatible with the claim that 'priority' is a *pros hen* equivocal, since all that is strictly necessary for this concept to have such a logical (and metaphysical) structure is that there be some one principal meaning to which the others are referred or reduced; cf. Owen 1960, pp. 163–90.

6. In the light of our discussion of Theta 8, however, we might regard it as somewhat tautologous if Aristotle were to say that substance is prior with respect to actuality, given that substance was there established as the principal sense of actuality.

7. Perhaps the best reason for treating priority and posteriority as *pros hen* equivocals is that they belong to the list of opposites Aristotle gives as general attributes of being that must be studied by any science of being qua being; cf. *Met.* IV, 2, 1005a13–18; III, 1, 995b18–25.

8. Owens (1951, p. 320) notes that Aristotle gives no reason why priority in time should be expressed in terms of separateness, though he himself has no difficulty in constructing a link between separability and temporal priority. It is such lacunae in explanation that prompt Owens to remark that Aristotle makes little effort to preserve the systematic divisions of priority.

9. For what it is worth, it should be noted that Ps. Alexander (*In Metaph.* 460,31ff. [Hayduck] offers a similar interpretation, using as his example the priority in time of a wine jar to the wine by analogy with a substance and the accidents that inhere in it. He concludes with an appeal to the criterion of nonreciprocal destruction that would presumably show that in each case the container is prior in substance and in time to the things contained. Aquinas

(*In Metaph.* VII, L.1, c.1257) follows the same line when he explains that substance is prior in time because none of the other predicates is separable from substance, while it alone is separable from the others.

10. See the recent exchange between Gail Fine and Donald Morrison about this terminology; cf. Fine 1984, pp. 31–87; Morrison 1985a, pp. 89–105, 1985b, pp. 167–73.

11. Ross (1924 ii, p. 160) thinks that an explanation of priority in time is to be found at 1028a33–34, since whatever can exist without other things while they cannot exist without it may naturally be said to exist before other things. But he is puzzled by the fact that this sense of priority was elsewhere distinguished from priority in time (cf. *Cat.* 14a26–35 and *Phy.* 260b18), as priority κατὰ φύσιν καὶ οὐσίαν—cf. *Met.* 1018b14, 1019a2. The London Group (1979, pp. 4ff.) is also puzzled by the obscure explanation of temporal priority and three possibilities were canvassed without a definite conclusion being reached. The third possibility suggested is similar to my explanation in proposing a context of change for viewing the question, so that for any quality its existence is seen as the result of change involving a preexisting substance.

12. The London Group seems to opt for the stronger claim that a *logos* of any quality must include a *logos* of substance; cf. Burnyeat 1979, pp. 5–6. But it is difficult to see how this could be held to conform with Aristotle's practice in defining qualities, unless we put a great deal of weight on his 'snub' example in Zeta 4 and 5. In that discussion, however, what Aristotle denies is that qualitative forms like snubness can be defined because, in the strict sense, there is definition only of substantial forms. Yet eventually he concedes that entities belonging to other categories may be defined, though not in a primary sense; cf. *Met.* 1030b3ff. Aristotle's point in using 'the snub' as a paradigm is that such physical forms cannot be defined without reference to the material substratum (or logical subject) to which they belong *per se.*

13. Aquinas (*In Metaph.* VII, L. 1, c.1258) draws an interesting parallel between the priority of substance over attributes, with respect to definition, and the priority of the genus animal over the species, man, since the definition of animal is presupposed in the definition of man.

14. Cf. Nehamas 1987, pp. 275–316. At *Met.* 993b23–31, I think we can find an application of the general Platonic principle that a secondary instantiation 'exists' and is knowable in virtue of a primary and paradigmatic form. For instance, fire has the quality of heat in the highest degree (μάλιστα) because in virtue of it the synonymous quality belongs to other things. In fact, this example provides a nice analogy for the intensity interpretation of the degrees-of-being thesis that Donald Morrison (MS 1) tends to espouse.

15. We should note that Aquinas implicitly appeals to the Aristotelian categories in order to explain the priority in knowledge of substance; cf. *In Metaph.* VII, L.1, c.1259.

16. For a more detailed discussion of the impasse being explored in Zeta 13, see Cleary 1987.

17. Ross (1924 ii, p. 210–11) thinks that γενέσει is added merely as a synonym of χρόνῳ .

18. At Zeta 15, 1040a18ff., Aristotle rehearses what is clearly a Platonic argument for the priority in being (τῷ εἶναι) of genus and differentia over the species based on the criterion of nonreciprocal destruction. I think that such an argument is representative of the position that he is attacking when he denies that a universal can be substantial.

19. *Met.* VI, 1, 1026a23–32: translation by Apostle 1966.

20. Cf. Merlan (1954, p. 160) accepts Eisler's historical claim that this terminology is the legacy of an otherwise obscure figure called Micraelius. He notes also that the distinction between *ens perfectissimum* and *ens commune* was accepted as well established by late medieval commentators like Petrus Fonseca. In spite of this long tradition, however, Merlan does not think that Aristotle himself was responsible for the distinction in such terms. In fact, he suggests (1954, p. 169) that Aristotle never distinguished general from special metaphysics, since he takes being-as-such not abstractly but rather as an element in all that is. Thus, according to Merlan, both *Metaphysics* Gamma and Epsilon were written within the tradition of Academic speculation that assumed there is at least one sphere of being beyond the sensible that is superior and also a causal element in the inferior. Perhaps there is a grain of truth in

Merlan's proposal, since Aristotle's position is formulated in terms of the prior and the posterior, though there are reasons to believe that he adapted this Platonic topic to his own purposes.

21. πότερον ποθ' ἡ πρώτη φιλοσοφία καθόλου ἐστιν—*Met.* 1026a23–24.

22. Patzig (1979, pp. 33–49) thinks that a resolution of the impasse depends on understanding the metaphysical relationship in virtue of which what holds true of the primary thing holds true universally.

23. Kirwan (1971, p. 188) thinks that the comparison with mathematics speaks only for the existence of general metaphysics and does nothing to reconcile this with special metaphysics. But this seems to underestimate the influence of the theory of proportion on Aristotle's metaphysical thought, given that it provides him with a leading example of a theory that is simultaneously universal and particular insofar as it can be applied to particular species of quantity. Kirwan may mean, however, that the general theory of proportion fails to give an exact parallel with a universal discipline that has a special application to a particular kind of being (e.g. a particular species of quantity). But this failure may be simply due to the loss of a focal meaning within the category of quantity when the Pythagorean schema, according to which numbers are prior, must be abandoned with the discovery of incommensurability.

24. It is worth noting that *Metaphysics* Gamma 2 spells out the comparison more clearly in terms of primary and secondary (δευτέρα) parts of mathematics; cf. 1004a6–9. Since any such ordering of the mathematical sciences would be made with reference to their characteristic objects, it is possible that some Pythagorean schema lies in the background here. But on the other hand, it is also worth considering the possibility that Aristotle thought of the general theory of proportion as the first of the mathematical sciences because it has both universal and particular applications.

25. Kirwan (1971, p. 187) notes that we are not told why the discipline whose objects are changeless and separable must be prior to all others, yet he conjectures that it must be because these objects themselves are prior. By way of explanation as to why such objects are prior, he offers the following Aristotelian considerations: (i) Only concrete substances are separable; cf. *Phy.* I, 2, 185a31. (ii) Substances are prior to all other things; cf. *Met.* Z 1, 1028a29–b2. (iii) Changeless substances are prior to other substances, since changers are prior to the things they change, changeless changers are prior to everything else; cf. *Met.* XII, 8, 1073a23–36. But, in spite of Kirwan's efforts, it is clear that only the third consideration is directly relevant to the question of whether there is a first philosophy distinct from physics, and even in this case, the exact sense of priority needs to be clarified.

26. Yet Ross (1924 i, p. 356) seems to think that the argument is fairly straightforward. Theology is more to be chosen than the other theoretical sciences; for if the question be asked whether it is universal or studies one particular kind of being, our answer is that it studies the primary kind of being, and that which gives their fundamental character to all other beings. Theology is thus both primary and universal, and doubly supreme among the sciences. It is difficult to see what clarification Ross has added, beyond repeating Aristotle's view in different terms. Kirwan (1971, p. 188) makes a better attempt when he explains that, in so far as it is ontology, metaphysics is both general and special because it explores the ways in which all beings depend on and refer to primary beings. But this gives him a very narrow conception of 'ontology,' and so he concludes that metaphysics is wider because it discusses the transcendentals and also logical principles.

27. Some commentators think that no satisfactory solution to this *aporia* is to be found in Aristotle's work and hence the controversy in later antiquity about his definitive view on the question; cf. Eslick 1957, p. 253.

28. Cf. *In Metaph.* 447,25ff. (Hayduck)

29. *Met.* IV, 2, 1003b16–19: translation by Kirwan 1971.

30. Ross (1924 i, p. 254) mentions substance briefly in his summary but provides no special note on this passage. Kirwan (1971, p. 81) recognizes that some principle of priority is being cited to support the statement that substance is prior, but he does not connect this

argument with what has gone before.

31. Though he is correct in referring to Zeta 1 as a parallel passage, Kirwan (1971, p. 81) seems to be mistaken in his claim that only priority in formula (as outlined in Zeta 1) is being appealed to here in Gamma 2. As far as I can see, there is very little verbal similarity between the criterion cited in Zeta 1 and the two distinct criteria cited in Gamma 2.

32. *Met.* IV, 2, 1004a2-9: translation by Kirwan 1971.

33. Cf. Owen 1965, pp. 125-50, 1975, pp. 14-34.

34. ἂν καθόλου λέγῃ τις καὶ κατ' ἀναλογίαν—*Met.* 1070a32.

35. Lambda 1 gives two ways in which substance is prior: (*a*) if the universe is a whole, substance will be the first part; whereas (*b*) if the universe is a series then substance will be first before quality and quantity, since none of these is separated (χωριστόν); cf. *Met.* 1069a19-21.

36. Adopting medieval terminology, we might call this proportional analogy to distinguish it from attributive analogy that was attached to the notion of a *pros hen* equivocal. But perhaps we should not make the common assumption that Aristotle himself had a *doctrine* about the analogy of being; cf. Aubenque 1986, pp. 35-46.

37. This lack of parallelism would seem to indicate that the analogical sameness of principles and elements being argued for in Lambda 4 and 5 applies only to sensible substance and its attributes.

38. In his review of opinions at Lambda 1, Aristotle says that the Platonists posit universals as being more substantial (οὐσίας μᾶλλον) because, according to their dialectical mode of inquiry (τὸ λογικῶς ζητεῖν), universal genera are more real as principles; cf. *Met.* 1069a26-28. This report illustrates how the degrees-of-being thesis was associated with priority in the Platonic tradition.

39. καὶ ὡδὶ τὰ τῶν οὐσιῶν αἴτια ὡς αἴτια πάντων—*Met.* 1071a34-35.

40. At the beginning of Lambda 5, Aristotle distinguishes substances as separated (or separable) things from those things that are not separated (οὐ χωριστά) and argues on this basis that the causes of all things are the same; cf. 1070b36ff. By way of justifying this conclusion, he explains that the attributes and motions would not 'exist' without the substances (ὅτι τῶν οὐσιῶν ἄνευ οὐκ ἔστι τὰ πάθη καὶ αἱ κινήσεις); cf. 1071a1-2. This explanation seems to contain an implicit appeal to a criterion of nonreciprocal dependence that would make substances prior by nature to their dependent attributes. Aristotle appears to regard such priority as a basis for the sameness of principles that, he suggests, might turn out to be soul and body or even nous and desire and body; cf. 1071a2-3. But these principles do not have the same level of generality as potency and act or even as matter, form, and privation. Thus it is difficult to see how they could be the same by analogy for all categories of being rather than belonging especially to living things as the primary instances of being. Even if they had the requisite generality, however, they would have to supply a different kind of analogy for the so-called πρὸς ἕν equivocal; e.g. analogy to the same terminus, as distinct from the analogy of proportionality; cf. Brentano 1862 and 1975, pp. 58-66; Philippe 1969, p. 27.

41. ὅτι ἀνάγκη εἶναι ἀίδιόν τινα οὐσίαν ἀκίνητον—*Met.* 1071b4.

42. Perhaps we could avoid these difficulties if we concentrate on the claim that the first mover is the cause of all things; cf. *Met.* 1070b34-35. If the Prime Mover itself is an unanalyzable simple, then it is a mistake to ask about its material cause or to try distinguishing between its formal and final causes.

43. Another outstanding problem that I have not tried to resolve is whether there is a special sense of "universal" that Aristotle uses when he claims that something is universal because it is prior. This was a problem that was discussed in great detail by medieval thinkers; cf. John Duns Scotus in Wolter (tr.) 1966.

44. Cf. *Phaedr.* 245C, *Laws* 849E, *Tim.* 34B. Ross (1924 ii, pp. 370-71) notes that Aristotle seems to be reasoning from the late point at which the formation of the soul appears in the *Timaeus,* even though Timaeus is made to explain that it is later only in the order of exposition. The crux of the matter appears to be that he describes soul as made by the God who finds the disordered movement as something preexisting; so that soul cannot be the cause of

this motion. But it is rather odd that Aristotle should so pointedly ignore the distinctions between different senses of priority that are made within the same context (*Tim.* 34C), especially since he is arguing that Plato treated the soul as both prior and posterior.

45. My argumentative strategy is supported by a remark that Aristotle makes at the beginning of *Physics* VII (ch. 1) when he introduces the question of whether or not motion exists eternally. He stresses that asking such a question is useful not only for the investigation of nature but also for the inquiry into the first principle (περὶ τῆς ἀρχῆς τῆς πρώτης); cf. 251a5–8.

46. *Phy.* VIII, 7, 260a23–26: translation by Apostle 1969.

47. I am grateful to Helen Lang for pointing out (in personal correspondence) that *Physics* VIII forms such a strong unity of argument that Aristotle may be taken to have proved the eternality of motion in chapter 1.

48. Simplicius (*In Phys.* 1265, 15ff. [Diels]) takes this argument to show that locomotion is prior by nature (κατὰ φύσιν) to the other kinds of change presumably because he finds in Aristotle's formulation an implicit criterion of nonreciprocal destruction. I think we can also find such a criterion hidden in the passage at *Physics* 260b4–5 that says: ταῦτα δ᾽ ἄνευ φορᾶς οὐκ ἐνδέχεται ὑπάρχειν.

49. Simplicius names Democritus and Anaxagoras and Empedocles as thinkers who shared the view that generation and corruption are somehow due to condensation and rarefaction; cf. *In Phys.* 1266,33ff. (Diels).

50. Cf. *Phy.* 204b4–11 for a similar distinction between an inquiry conducted "logically" (λογικῶς) and one that proceeds "physically" (φυσικῶς).

51. *Phy.* VIII, 7, 260b17–19: translation by Apostle 1969.

52. In the previous chapter this assumption seems to be linked with a principle of economy; i.e. that we should always posit a finite number of principles for natural things because what is finite and better (τὸ βέλτιον) should exist to a higher degree (μᾶλλον) where this is possible; cf. *Phy.* VIII, 6, 259a10–13.

53. τὸ δὲ βέλτιον ἀεὶ ὑπολαμβάνομεν ἐν τῇ φύσει ὑπάρχειν, ἂν ᾖ δυνατόν—*Phy.* 260b22–23.

54. *Phy.* VIII, 7, 260b26–29: translation by Apostle (1969) with his insertions in parentheses. I cannot account for his failure to translate the word ἀλλοιοῦσθαι or for his insertion of "decreasing" as a correspondent to "increasing" without any warrant from the Greek text.

55. Indeed, Simplicius (*In Phys.* 1269,23–28 [Diels]) uses the formulation from the *Categories* to elucidate the criterion of nonreciprocal dependence that is being applied by Aristotle here.

56. ἀριθμὸς κινήσεως κατὰ τὸ πρότερον καὶ ὕστερον—*Phy.* IV, 11, 219b1–2.

57. Simplicius (*In Phys.* 1270,7 ff.) finds the conclusion quite intelligible because, just as eternal things are prior in time to generated things, so it is also with motion; i.e. that which belongs to things that are eternally moved is prior to that which belongs to generated things that cannot be eternally moved.

58. πάντα γὰρ ἂν εἴη τὰ κινούμενα φθαρτά—*Phy.* 261a8–9.

59. This provides us with another example of the claim in *Metaphysics* Epsilon 1 that something is universal because it is prior. Once again, the claim can be seen to depend on the fact that the many senses of 'motion' have a primary or focal meaning; i.e. that it has the logical structure of a *pros hen* equivocal.

60. Simplicius (*In Phys.* 1270,35–37) claims that the locomotion of the sun is prior in time to any individual perishable thing because of being one of its ultimate causes.

61. ὥστε τὸ τῇ γενέσει ὕστερον τῇ φύσει πρότερον εἶναι—*Phy.* 261a13–14.

62. εἰ μᾶλλον ὑπάρχει φορὰ τοῖς μᾶλλον ἀπειληφόσιν τὴν φύσιν—*Phy.* 261a18–19.

63. ἡ κίνησις αὕτη πρώτη τῶν ἄλλων ἂν εἴη κατ᾽ οὐσίαν—*Phy.* 261a19–20.

64. ὅτι τὸ κινοῦν αὐτὸ αὐτὸ μάλιστα ταύτην κινεῖ κυρίως, τὴν κατὰ τόπον—*Phy.* 261a23–24.

65. Cf. *Phaedrus* 245C5–246A2. Simplicius (*In Phys.* 1272,38–1273,12) thinks that, in order to make his argument, Aristotle is here drawing upon Plato's *Laws,* Book X.

66. Like other modern commentators, Ross (1936, p. 709ff.) obviously grasps the general line of argument in this chapter but unaccountably fails to give an adequate account of the

central role that the different senses of priority play in the whole argument.

67. On this subject it is noteworthy that Aristotle's first argument for the priority of circular over rectilinear locomotion begins with an appeal to the criterion of greater simplicity and completeness; cf. *Phy.* VIII, 9, 265a13ff. Subsequently, he claims that what is complete is prior in nature (φύσει) and in definition (λόγῳ) and in time (χρόνῳ) to what is incomplete. Similarly, what is indestructible is prior (in all of these ways) to what is destructible, just as those things which can be eternal are prior to those things that cannot. But he argues, only a circular locomotion can be eternal and indestructible, so it is prior (in every way) to rectilinear motion. Given the whole context, the hidden implication of the argument is that this is the most appropriate motion to be caused by the Prime Mover.

68. *Met.* XIII, 2, 1077a14–20: translation by Apostle 1966.

69. εἴ τις θήσει οὕτως εἶναι τὰ μαθηματικῶς κεχωρισμένας τινὰ φύσεις. . .—*Met.* 1077a 15–16.

70. τοὐναντίον συμβαίνει καὶ τοῦ εἰωθότος ὑπολαμβάνεσθαι—*Met.* 1077a14–15. Annas (1976, p. 144) thinks that "ordinary beliefs" are being appealed to here, since she claims that for Aristotle a *prima facie* objection to the Academy's theories is that they would lead us to say counterintuitive things about the reality of numbers as well as of tables and other concrete things.

71. Annas (1976, p. 144) reads the argument as appealing to the notion of completeness and as claiming that physical objects have "ontological priority" over the abstract objects studied by mathematics. Unfortunately, however, this could correspond to at least two of Aristotle's many senses of priority, depending on how the criterion of completeness is applied, so that her interpretation is ambiguous.

72. Ross (1924 ii, p. 414) follows Bonitz (1849) in claiming that there is a serious ambiguity in Aristotle's use of γένεσις in this argument, since the criterion of priority applicable to natural generation can hardly be applied to the different process by which a line is 'generated.' Still, if the same ambiguity were present in Plato's thought, Aristotle's argument would constitute an effective dialectical refutation.

73. Ross (1924 ii, p. 414) thinks that there is also an ambiguity in the meaning of τῇ οὐσίᾳ πρότερον throughout Mu 2; i.e. that there are at least two senses that answer to two meanings of οὐσία often distinguished by Aristotle: (i) form or the τόδε τι considered as a fully formed thing; (ii) τὸ ὑποκείμενον or the τόδε τι considered as capable of separate existence. But I think that Ross misses the dialectical play upon this ambiguity, which depends upon applying different criteria of priority or even the same criterion in different contexts.

74. *Met.* XIII, 2, 1077a24–31: translation by Apostle 1966.

75. Cf. *Laws* X, 894A–B, which seems to describe such a 'generation' of perceptible body in three stages.

76. Proclus, *In Eucl.* 77.16ff–cf. Morrow 1970, pp. 63ff.

77. τελευταῖον δ' εἰς βάθος, καὶ τέλος ἔσχεν—*Met.* 1077a25–26.

78. τὸ τῇ γενέσει ὕστερον τῇ οὐσίᾳ πρότερον—*Met.* 1077a26–27.

79. Perhaps the argument is pointedly directed against the well-known Platonic tendency to associate mathematical objects, especially numbers, with the soul; cf. *DA* 1, 2, 404b16–27.

80. Annas (1976, p. 146) thinks he is not playing fair because he acknowledges elsewhere that the 'generation' of mathematical objects has a different meaning from that applied to physical objects, since lines and surfaces 'come to be' without there being anything from which they come as must be the case for physical objects. But the dialectical passage to which she refers (cf. *Met.* 1002a28–b5) does nothing to show that the Platonists had already distinguished this kind of generation from that of ordinary sensible things. On the contrary, it lists further difficulties for their view that mathematical objects are substances.

81. *Met.* XIII, 2, 1077a36–b11: translated by Apostle 1966.

82. ἀλλ' οὐ πάντα ὅσα τῷ λόγῳ πρότερα καὶ τῇ οὐσίᾳ οὐ πρότερα—*Met.* 1077b1–2.

83. If we apply this criterion to the Prime Mover as a candidate for supersensible substance, it is likely that it would qualify as being prior in substance to sensible substances. This provides confirmation of Aristotle's acceptance of a certain hierarchical ordering among sub-

stances, in spite of what he says elsewhere to the contrary; cf. *Met.* VII, 12, 1038a33–35.

84. Annas (1976, p. 147) suggests that he may be making a distinct point about what she calls the "ontological priority" of mathematical objects to physical objects as counted, measured, etc. Thus, on her account, the former would be prior in definition because to define something as X inches long is to employ the concept of length, which itself is already defined independently of particular exemplifications. Annas thinks that Aristotle is willing to grant this because it does not threaten the "ontological priority" of the individual measured. In addition to the ambiguity of the phrase "ontological priority," her interpretation is undercut by the fact that in Zeta 1 Aristotle takes priority in definition to have ontological implications in the sense of priority in substance.

85. By contrast, Syrianus (*In Metaph.* 93,21ff. [Kroll]) assumes that the same sense of λόγος is operative here and he argues that, according to the criteria proposed in Zeta, mathematical objects should really be prior to sensibles, not only in definition but also in substance, since they surpass them in being (τῷ γὰρ εἶναι ὑπερβάλλει). Of course, we should understand this interpretation to be motivated by the desire of a Platonist to stand Aristotle on his head, using the same dialectical strategy as he used on the Master.

86. κατὰ τὸν λόγον δὲ τὸ συμβεβηκὸς τοῦ ὅλου πρότερον—*Met.* 1018b34–35.

87. καίτοι οὐκ ἐνδέχεται μουσικὸν εἶναι μὴ ὄντος μουσικοῦ τινός—*Met.* 1018b36–37.

88. οὐ γὰρ ἐνδέχεται εἶναι κεχωρισμένον ἀλλ᾽ ἀεὶ ἅμα τῷ συνόλῳ ἐστίν—*Met.* 1077b7–8. This passage contains one of the few examples in Aristotle's mature work where the word ἅμα is used by way of contrast with πρότερον in an ontological sense and, significantly enough, it is used to deny the separability that is associated with priority in substance; cf. also *Met.* 1071b37–1072a3.

89. For an analysis of the meaning of terms like 'abstraction' in this passage, see Cleary 1985, pp. 26–30.

90. In spite of their long notes on this point, both Ross (1924 ii, 414) and Annas (1976, p. 146) seem to be confused about the precise senses of priority involved in the argument.

91. I am not assuming that Aristotle still holds the particular sensible thing, as an object of perception, to be the primary substance. My point is that, even if biological form be given that privileged status, its functioning or activity must be first ascertained through sense experience rather than through the abstract mathematical reasoning that characterized the Academic approach to substance.

BIBLIOGRAPHY

Texts

Aristotle: De Anima. R. D. Hicks, ed. and comm. 1907. Cambridge: Cambridge University Press.
Aristotle: Posterior Analytics (H. Tredennick, tr.) with *Topica* (E. S. Forster, tr.). G. P. Goold, ed. 1960. Vol. 2. Loeb series. Cambridge: Harvard University Press.
Aristotle's Categories and De Interpretatione. J. L. Ackrill, tr. and comm. 1963. Oxford: Clarendon.
Aristotle's Categories and Propositions. H. G. Apostle, tr. and notes. 1980. Iowa: Peripatetic.
Aristotle's Metaphysics. H. G. Apostle, tr. and notes. 1966. Bloomington: Indiana University.
Aristotle's Metaphysics. W. D. Ross, ed. and notes. 1924. 2 vols. Oxford: Clarendon.
Aristotle's Metaphysics: Books Γ, Δ, and E. C. Kirwan, tr. and comm. 1971. Oxford: Clarendon.
Aristotle's Metaphysics: Books M and N. J. Annas, tr. and comm. 1976. Oxford: Clarendon.
Aristotle's Physics. H. G. Apostle, tr. and notes. 1969. Bloomington: Indiana University Press.
Aristotle's Physics. W. D. Ross, ed. and comm. 1936. Oxford: Clarendon.
Aristotle's Posterior Analytics. J. Barnes, tr. and comm. 1975. Oxford: Clarendon.
Aristotelis, Fragmenta Selecta. W. D. Ross, ed. 1955. Oxford: Clarendon.
Aristotelis Metaphysica. H. Bonitz, ed. 1849; rpt. 1960. 2 vols. Hildesheim: Olms
Aristotelis Metaphysica. W. Jaeger, ed. 1957. Oxford: Clarendon.
Aristotelis Organon Graece. T. Waitz, ed. 1844, 1846. 2 vols. Leipzig: Hahn.
Aristotelis Physica. W. D. Ross, ed. 1950. Oxford: Clarendon.
Platonis Opera. J. Burnet, ed. 1900–1904. 5 vols. Oxford: Clarendon.
Select Fragments. W. D. Ross, tr. 1952. In *The Works of Aristotle,* vol. 12. Oxford: Clarendon.
The Works of Aristotle. W. D. Ross, ed. 1928. Vol. 1. Oxford: Oxford University Press.

Commentaries

Commentaria in Aristotelem Graeca. Prussian Academy, ed. 1882–1909. 23 vols. Berlin: Reimeri.
———. Alexander. *In Aristotelis Metaphysica Commentaria.* M. Hayduck, ed. 1891. Vol. I.
———. Alexander. *In Aristotelis Topicorum Commentaria.* M. Wallies, ed. 1891. Vol. II, par. 2.
———. Olympiodorus. *Prolegomena et in Categorias Commentarium.* A. Busse, ed. 1902. Vol. XII, par. 1.
———. Philoponus. *In Aristotelis Categorias Commentarium.* A. Busse, ed. 1898. Vol. XIII, par. 1.
———. Philoponus. *In Aristotelis Analytica Posteriora Commentaria.* M. Wallies, ed. 1909. Vol. XIII, par. 2.
———. Simplicius. *In Aristotelis Categorias Commentarium.* C. Kalbfleisch, ed. 1907. Vol. VIII.
———. Simplicius. *In Aristotelis Physicorum.* H. Diels, ed. 1882. Vols. IX-X.
———. Syrianus. *In Metaphysica Commentaria.* G. Kroll, ed. 1902. Vol. VI, par. 1.
———. Themistius. *Paraphrasis in Analytica Posteriora.* M. Wallies, ed. 1900. Vol. V, par. 1.
Eudoxus von Knidos. F. Lasserre, ed. and comm. 1966. *Texte und Kommentare.* Band 4. Berlin: De Gruyter.
Proclus, *A Commentary on the First Book of Euclid's Elements.* G. R. Morrow, tr. and notes. 1970. Princeton: Princeton University Press.

Straton von Lampsakos. F. Wehrli, ed. 1969. *Die Schule des Aristoteles.* Heft V. Basel: Schwabe.
Thomas Aquinas. *In Metaphysicam Aristotelis Commentaria.* M.-R. Cathala, ed. 1926. Turin: Marietta.

Secondary Literature

Anton, J. P. 1957. *Aristotle's Theory of Contrareity.* London: Routledge and Kegan Paul.
Apelt, O. 1891. *Beiträge zur Geschichte der griechischen Philosophie.* Leipzig: Weidmann.
Arpe, C. 1938. *Das τί ἦν εἶναι bei Aristoteles.* Hamburg: De Gruyter.
Ast, T. 1835, rpt. 1956. *Lexicon Platonicum.* 3 vols. Bonn: Habelt.
Aubenque, P. 1962. *Le problème de l'être chez Aristote.* Paris: Presses Universitaires.
_____. 1986. "The Origins of the Doctrine of the Analogy of Being." *Graduate Faculty Philosophy Journal* 11:35–46.
Barnes, J., ed. 1975 and 1979. *Articles on Aristotle.* Vols. 1 and 3. London: Duckworth.
_____. 1982. *Aristotle.* Oxford: Oxford University Press.
_____. 1985. "Aristotelian Arithmetic." *Revue de Philosophie Ancienne* 3:97–133.
Boehner, P., ed. and tr. 1957. *Ockham, Philosophical Writings.* Edinburgh: Nelson.
Bonitz, H. 1870. *Index Aristotelicum.* Berlin: Reimeri.
Boyer, C. B. 1968. *A History of Mathematics.* New York: Wiley.
Brandwood, L. 1976. *A Word Index to Plato.* Leeds: Maney.
Brentano, F. 1862. *Von der mannigfachen Bedeutung des Seienden nach Aristoteles.* Freiburg: Herder. (Translated, *On the Several Senses of Being in Aristotle,* by R. George. Berkeley: University of California Press, 1975.)
Burnyeat, M., ed. 1979. *Notes on Book Zeta of Aristotle's Metaphysics.* Oxford: Philosophy.
Busa, R., ed. 1975. *Sancti Thomae Aquinatis Operum Omnium Indices et Concordanti.* Stuttgart: Frommann-Holzboog.
Callahan, J. F. 1948. *Four Views on Time in Ancient Philosophy.* Cambridge: Harvard University Press.
Cherniss, H. 1944. *Aristotle's Criticism of Plato and the Academy.* Baltimore: Johns Hopkins.
_____. 1945. *The Riddle of the Early Academy.* Berkeley: University of California Press.
Cleary, J. J. 1985. "On the Terminology of 'Abstraction' in Aristotle." *Phronesis* 30:13–45.
_____. 1987. "Science, Universals and Reality." *Ancient Philosophy* 7:95–130.
Cook, Wilson, J. 1904. "On the Platonist Doctrine of the ἀσύμβλητοι ἀριθμοί." *Classical Review* 18:247–60.
Corish, D. 1976. "Aristotle's Attempted Derivation of Temporal Order from That of Movement and Space." *Phronesis* 21:241–51.
De Raeymaeker, L. 1935. *Metaphysica Generalis.* Vol. 1. London.
De Rijk, L. M. 1951. "The Authenticity of the *Categories." Mnemosyne* 4:129–59.
_____. 1952. *The Place of the Categories of Being in Aristotle's Philosophy.* Assen: Van Gorcum.
Duns Scotus, John. *Opus Oxoniense.* T. IX, *Opera Omina.* L. Wadding, ed. Paris: Vives, 1893.
_____. *A Treatise on God as First Principle.* A. B. Wolter, tr. Chicago: Franciscan Herald, 1966.
Eslick, L. E. 1957. "What Is the Starting Point of Metaphysics?" *Modern Schoolman* 34:247–63.
Evans, J. D. G. 1977. *Aristotle's Concept of Dialectic.* Cambridge: Cambridge University Press.
Fine, G. 1984. "Separation." *Oxford Studies in Ancient Philosophy* 2:31–87.
Frede, M. 1981. "Categories in Aristotle." In D. J. O'Meara, ed., *Studies in Aristotle,* pp. 1–24. Washington: Catholic University Press.
_____. 1983. "Titel, Einheit und Echtheit der Kategorien." In Moraux and Wiesner, eds., *Zweifelhaftes im Corpus Aristotelicum,* pp. 1–29. Berlin: De Gruyter. (Translated, "The Title, Unity, and Authenticity of the Aristotelian *Categories,"* in *Essays in Ancient Philosophy,* pp. 11–28. Minneapolis: University of Minnesota Press, 1987.)

Furley, D. J. 1967. *Two Studies in the Greek Atomists.* Princeton: Princeton University Press.

Furth, M. 1978. "Transtemporal Stability in Aristotelian Substances." *Journal of Philosophy* 75: 624–46.

Gadamer, H.-G. 1978. *Die Idee des Guten zwischen Plato und Aristoteles.* Heidelberg: Winter. (Translated, *The Idea of the Good in Platonic-Aristotelian Philosophy*, by C. Smith. New Haven: Yale University Press, 1986.)

Gaiser, K. 1962. *Platons ungeschriebene Lehre.* Stuttgart: Klett.

Gram, M. S. 1968. *Kant, Ontology, and the A Priori.* Evanston: Northwestern University Press.

Grayeff, F. 1974. *Aristotle and His School.* London: Duckworth.

Hambruch, E. 1904. *Logische Regeln der platonischen Schule in der aristotelischen Topik.* Berlin: Weidmann.

Hamlyn, D. W. 1978. "Focal Meaning." *Proceedings of the Aristotelian Society* 78:1–18.

Heath, T. L. 1921. *A History of Greek Mathematics.* Oxford: Clarendon.

———. 1925. *The Thirteen Books of Euclid's Elements.* 3 vols. Cambridge: Cambridge University Press.

———. 1949. *Mathematics in Aristotle.* Oxford: Clarendon.

Irwin, T. H. 1982. "Aristotle's Concept of Signification." In Schofield and Nussbaum, eds., *Language and Logos,* pp. 241–66. Cambridge: Cambridge University Press.

Jaeger, W. 1923. *Aristoteles, Grundlegung einer Geschichte seiner Entwicklung.* Berlin: Weidmann. (Translated, *Aristotle: Fundamentals of the History of His Development,* by R. Robinson. Oxford: Oxford University Press, 1934.)

Kahn, C. H. 1973. *The Verb 'Be' in Ancient Greek.* Dordrecht/Boston: D. Reidel.

———. 1976. "Why Existence Does Not Emerge as a Distinct Concept in Greek Philosophy." *Archiv für Geschichte der Philosophie* 58:323–34.

Klein, J. 1968. *Greek Mathematical Thought and the Origin of Algebra.* E. Brann, tr. Cambridge: M.I.T. Press.

Kung, J. 1986. "Aristotle on 'Being Is Said in Many Ways.' " *History of Philosophy Quarterly* 3:3–18.

Liddell, H.; Scott, R.; and Jones, J. 1925. *A Greek-English Lexicon.* Oxford: Clarendon.

Lloyd, A. C. 1962. "Genus, Species and Ordered Series in Aristotle." *Phronesis* 7:67–90.

Mansion, S. 1979. "Plus Connu en Soi', 'Plus Connu pour nous.' Une distinction epistemologique importante chez Aristote." *Pensamiento* 35:161–70.

Merlan, P. 1975. *From Platonism to Neoplatonism.* The Hague: Nijhoff.

Moraux, P. 1973. *Der Aristotelismus bei den Griechen.* Vol. 1. Berlin: De Gruyter.

Morrison, D. 1985a "*Choristos* in Aristotle." *Harvard Studies in Classical Philology* 89:89–105

———. 1985b. "Separation: A Reply to Fine." *Oxford Studies in Ancient Philosophy* 3:167–73.

———. MS 1: "Aristotle's Theory of Degrees of Being."

———. 1987. "The Evidence for Degrees of Being in Aristotle." *Classical Quarterly* 37:382–401.

Mutschmann, H. 1906. *Divisiones quae vulgo dicuntur Aristoteleae.* Leipzig: Teubner.

Nehamas, A. 1987. "Socratic Intellectualism." In J. J. Cleary, ed., *Proceedings of the Boston Area Colloquium in Ancient Philosophy* 2:275–316. Lanham: University Press of America.

Nicol, A. 1936. "Indivisible Lines." *Classical Quarterly* 30:120–26.

Owen, G. E. L. 1960. "Logic and Metaphysics in Some Earlier Works of Aristotle." In During and Owen, eds., *Aristotle and Plato in the mid-Fourth Century,* pp. 163–90. Goteborg: Elanders.

———. 1965. "The Platonism of Aristotle," *Proceedings of the British Academy* 51:125–50.

Owens, J. 1951. *The Doctrine of Being in the Aristotelian Metaphysics.* Toronto: Pontifical Institute.

Patzig, G. 1979. "Theology and Ontology in Aristotle's *Metaphysics.*" In J. Barnes, ed., *Articles on Aristotle* 3:33–49. London: Duckworth.

Philippe, M.-D. 1969. "*Analogon* and *Analogia* in the Philosophy of Aristotle." *Thomist* 33:1–74

Reale, G. 1980. *The Concept of First Philosophy and the Unity of the Metaphysics of Aristotle.* J. R. Catan, tr. Albany: SUNY Press.

Rist, J. "The Mind of Aristotle. A Study in Philosophical Development." MS.
Robin, L. 1908. *La Théorie platonicienne des Idées et des Nombres d'après Aristote.* Paris: Presses Universitaires.
Szabo, A. 1978. *The Beginnings of Greek Mathematics.* Dordrecht/Boston: D. Reidel.
Taran, L. 1981. *Speusippus of Athens.* Leiden: Brill.
Vlastos, G. 1965. "Degrees of Reality in Plato." In G. Vlastos, ed., *Platonic Studies,* pp. 58–75. Princeton: Princeton University Press, 1973.
_____. 1966. "A Metaphysical Paradox." In G. Vlastos, ed., *Platonic Studies,* pp. 43–57. Princeton: Princeton University Press, 1973.
Wieland, W. 1960. "Das Problem der Prinzipienforschung und die aristotelische Physik." *Kant-Studien* 52:206–19. (Translated, "Aristotle's Physics and the Problem of Inquiry into Principles," in J. Barnes, ed., *Articles on Aristotle* 1:127–40. London: Duckworth, 1975.)
Wilpert, P. 1949. *Zwei aristotelische Fruhschriften uber die Ideenlehre.* Regensburg.
Wolter, A. B. 1946. *The Transcendentals and their Function in the Metaphysics of Duns Scotus.* New York: Franciscan Institute.
_____. tr. 1962. *Duns Scotus, Philosophical Writings.* Edinburgh: Nelson.

INDEX

JOHN J. CLEARY IS ASSOCIATE PROFESSOR OF PHILOSOPHY AT BOSTON College and was Director of the Boston Area Colloquium in Ancient Philosophy (BACAP) from 1983 to 1988. As editor of three volumes of the BACAP *Proceedings*, he has made innovative use of a Macintosh personal computer to produce camera-ready copy for the copublishers, University Press of America. He has also published journal articles in *Phronesis* and *Ancient Philosophy* and is presently preparing a book-length manuscript on "Aristotle and Mathematics." Dr. Cleary was educated at University College Dublin (B.A. and M.A.) and at Boston University (Ph.D.). A native of the Republic of Ireland, he is now a resident in the U.S.A.